This book offers a rare insight into the concept of halal and how business can utilise it effectively as a strategic tool to sell halal compliant products and services worldwide. The global halal market is a huge and lucrative market with which many western enterprises are unfamiliar or know little about. This book demystifies halal and tells you how this market works and what its requirements are. Abdul Ayan's presentation of how business can take advantage of the opportunities in this market is at once detailed, and simple. Highly informative and practical it sets out in a clear and forthright manner and with abundant examples how to produce and how not to produce halal as well as how to export to and operate in the global halal market. No other text has to date brought together all the elements necessary to operate in this market as Abdul Ayan does in this book. It is a very useful guide for business.

Abdul Ayan has taught Middle Eastern Studies and Arabic and Islamic cultures at the Universities of Melbourne and RMIT, respectively. He worked in community development establishing several Islamic community organisations in Australia. He has held many conferences on Middle East and halal trade. In 1995, 1996 and 1999 he held as the principal organiser three International halal conferences in Melbourne Australia, the earliest being arguably the first of its kind for business in the world. He has also advised the State Government of Victoria (2001-2007) on improving the State's export potential and is a consultant to Mr. Saad Al Shumaimry, the Director of the Muslim World League in Australia and New Zealand on halal issues. He is the principal of Aus-Halal Pty Ltd and has worked in the halal industry for nearly twenty years. He is currently a consultant on halal trade and commerce. Email a.ayan@bigpond.com

Accessing the Global Halal Market

Abdullahi Ayan

Abdullahi Ayan
Accessing the Global Halal Market

1st Edition
Includes index
Bibliography

Subjects: Business, Halal trade and commerce, Marketing, Halal standards & rules, Islamic culture, Islamic law.

No part of this publication may be reproduced, transmitted or stored in any form or by any means without the prior written permission of the copyright owner or the publisher. The distribution, scanning and uploading of this book via the internet without the permission of the publisher is illegal. Please make sure you purchase only authorised editions.

Copyright © 2013 Abdullahi Ayan

All rights reserved.

ISBN: 1479217778

ISBN 13: 9781479217779

Printed by Createspace, North Charleston, SC

Createspace estore page; www.createspace.com/3901685

To my family, my extended family and friends and to the memory of those among them who have passed away.

Contents

List of Tables and Figures	xi
Preface	xiii
Acknowledgements:	xv
Chapter 1 Producing Halal Food: Why, How and for whom?	1
Chapter 2 Responding to Consumer and Industry Trends through Halal Certification	13
Chapter 3 Meat and Livestock Australia's Global Halal Brand: A brand to be … or not to be	45
Chapter 4 Thinking Halal, Doing Halal: A Frame of Reference	67
Chapter 5 Prospects of Branding Halal: A Brunei initiative	93
Chapter 6 Halal Development: Beyond the Rubber-stamp Syndrome	121
Chapter 7 A Halal Inspection Report of PPP Pty Ltd.*	143
Chapter 8 Crisis in Australia's Live Cattle Exports to Indonesia: Where are the Solutions?	159

Glossary	165
References	169
Appendices	175
Index	193

List of Tables and Figures

Tables

Table 1
    Global halal food market size by region (US$)   17

Table 2
    Australian lamb & mutton exports for Dec. 2009   41

Table 3
    The countries that accredit certifiers in Australia and numbers they accredit in each State   53

Table 4
    Comparative Models: contrasting characteristics   135

Figures

Figures 1&2
    Weak and strong halal certification   23

Figure 3
    MLA's halal brand from its website (2012)   48

Figure 4
    Halal certification system: structure and functions   89

Preface

They ask thee what is lawful (or halal) to them as food.
Say: Lawful unto you are all things good, wholesome and
pure... (Al Quran 5:5).

They ask thee concerning wine [alcohol & drugs] and gambling.
Say: [O Prophet] In them there is great harm and some benefit
for human beings, but the harm (or sin) is far greater than the
benefit (Al Quran 2:219)

O ye who believe! Do not prohibit (make haram)
the good things which God has made halal (lawful) for you,
and do not transgress. Lo! God loves not transgressors.
(Al Quran 5:90-91).

Do you not see that God has subjected to your (use) all things
in the heavens and on earth, and has made His bounties flow to
you in exceeding measure, both seen and unseen...?
(Al Quran 31:20)

Acknowledgements

A special thanks to my wife Dr Margaret (Muna) McKenzie for her encouragement and support which kept up my enthusiasm for writing this book, and for reading the manuscript. I also wish to thank CRF Colac Pty Ltd in Victoria, Australia for the permission to use its approved halal operational manual to show how this kind of document may be formulated and presented. I am grateful to Dr. Ron Harper who has kindly advised me on how to get this book published. To Ali Chawk and Saad Al Shumaimry, Director of the Muslim World League in Australia and New Zealand, many thanks for the discussions I have had with them on halal issues such as halal reform and development which helped sharpen my ideas. I am grateful to the many Halal establishments that I have inspected or provided labour hire services to who have over the years broadened and deepened my understanding of how they apply the halal standard and produce halal compliant goods and services for the domestic and global halal market. To Professor Sheikh Yusuf Al-Qardawi whose ideas in his book *The lawful and the Prohibited in Islam* have inspired and guided me in writing this book my deep appreciation and gratitude. Finally I wish to thank all the authors whose works I acknowledge in the references contained herein. Any errors of omission or commission that may be found in this book are, of course, solely mine.

Introduction

Halal is a fundamental concept in Islam. In important ways, it gives insight into how Muslims see the world around them and act in it. Deeply rooted in Islamic law and doctrine it can also be part of other fields of study such as history, sociology, culture, communication and politics. This book, however, is not intended to be an academic or a religious treatise. It has a more practical and mundane orientation: conducting halal trade and commerce. It is particularly about how business enterprises can utilise the concept for this purpose in order to operate efficiently in and capture a significantly larger share of the global halal market than they currently do. To do so requires basic understanding of halal and how it can be used to produce and sell halal compliant goods and services by fulfilling prescribed halal requirements. This is the focus of this book. It is also about a complex of other related issues ranging from halal certification, halal branding, halal standards, and the norms and values that underpin them-issues that are key to influencing the purchasing decisions of global halal consumers.

Halal is a fast growing area of commerce. The current classification of the products to which it is applied are divided into halal food and non-food halal products (non-food includes cosmetics and personal care products, pharmaceuticals and other health products but excludes banking and financial products to which the concept also applies). The combined value of halal food and non-food halal products is estimated (circa 2006) to be worth more than $ 2 trillion globally. Although little known in the west until recently, the concept of halal is not new. Halal is at least as old as the advent of Islam and is by no means unfamiliar, albeit under a different guise, to both Christianity and Judaism-and particularly to Judaism in which it is extant and applied in practice under the term *Kosher*.

I have not thought about writing this book until quite recently, although many of its essays were written for and delivered at halal conference in Asia. Only in retrospect did I realise that it has been in gestation for a long time with its genesis going back to my teaching of modern Middle East and Arabic and Islamic Cultures at the University of Melbourne and RMIT University more than twenty years ago. But there were also other influences, among them my most recent experiences in the field of halal trade and commerce as a consultant and as a provider of labour hire services to halal establishments. But perhaps most important among these influences are the three International halal conferences I have held as principal organiser in Melbourne in 1995, 1996 and 1999 -with the earliest being arguably the first of its kind for business in the world. All these and other experiences have, to a greater or lesser extent, contributed to writing this book.

There are to my knowledge no books in English or any other language published in the field of halal for business enterprises-other than perhaps one or two self-published ones of which I am not aware. The main reason for writing this book is therefore to provide a useful reference and a practical guide which business can consult in their halal operations. In the absence of relevant information on halal, it offers better understanding of what halal is, how it can be utilised in the production of goods and services and how it can be rendered in the market place. The essays have been chosen to represent a wide range of halal issues of interest to business enterprises with the main aim of facilitating access to the global halal market. They also underscore the need for commitment by halal stakeholders to halal development and working towards a common purpose.

Chapter 1 deals with halal production and processes and in particular how firms can comply with a halal standard(s). It includes an abridged version of a halal standard of an actual certifier. It was published as part of a journal article I have written in *Food Australia*, The official journal of Australian Institute of Food Science and Technology (vol. 53 Number 11 November 2001). I wish to thank the publishers for their kind permission to reproduce it here, with minimal changes. It is important to make the point however that a halal standard is an instrument devised for the control and management of halal goods and services more commonly by Halal authorities than by halal certifiers. The two most important conditions for a business enterprise to meet are firstly, compliance with a prescribed halal standard (or set of standards) and secondly, the relevant establishment to have an approved halal program (or operational manual), consistent with that standard, to show how it does halal or how it would do it if it were an unregistered establishment seeking halal approval. Both of these conditions are discussed extensively under most topics.

Chapter 2 is perhaps the most important at least in the sense that it covers a much broader scope of halal issues than any of the other topics in this collection of essays. Among the major issues it discusses is the relationship of halal producers and halal consumers; a relationship mediated, given meaning and solidity by halal certification-without which the relationship would not exist. It identifies who halal consumers are and finds that their presumed identity and composition does not reflect current reality. This finding is significant and in recognition of that the term is redefined-albeit tentatively. Central to this redefinition is that halal consumers are not solely Muslim consumers as has been understood to be the case in the past but globally dispersed consumers who are both Muslim and non-Muslim. It argues that the identity of the non-Muslim halal consumers has never before been acknowledged but was ignored and excluded from the definition. Their recognition and acknowledgement is therefore long overdue. The essay however has a broader aim. It is to shows how the strategic use of the halal method can substantially increase demand for halal goods in the global marketplace. The success of this strategy is only possible, it is argued, through adopting halal certification.

Chapters 3 and 5 are about branding halal. They show separately how two firms one in Brunei and the other in Australia have created and utilised halal brands differently-conceptually and in practice. The former entity is the Brunei global halal brand and the latter is Meat and Livestock Australia's (MLA's) global halal brand. Other than the fact that they both claim to be brands they appear to share little else in common and have come to the brand landscape through different paths.

Chapter 5 on the Brunei global halal brand explores the rationale for its creation and what is proposed to be achieved by utlising it. It sets out the potential of the brand in the brand landscape and points both to the opportunities and challenges it may face as a specifically halal brand. It discusses also whether non-halal global brands can partly or wholly become halal brands or produce halal products and explores the obstacles they may face and how they may be able to overcome them- a discussion which revolves around whether they can assume a halal identity, gain credibility and adopt halal norms and values. In this context it points to the progress made in halal/ brand relationship and how that relationship can be constructed in different ways. It also identifies unresolved operational and logistical issues which stand in the way of its development as a halal brand. In the case of MLA brand, the main question is how the brand came to be, whether it is a legitimate halal brand or not and upon whose authority it has become a halal brand? The essay explores these issues and comes to the conclusion that it is not a halal brand in its current formulation and construction in the sense that it does not comply with halal norms and values. It proposes a pathway through which MLA can legitimise its band and give it a clear identity and credibility as a halal brand. As a paper it was first published in part in *The Halal Journal* issue 38 January & February 2011.

Chapter 4, "Thinking Halal, Doing Halal: A Frame of Reference", delineates the doctrinal and philosophical underpinnings of halal, what it means, the traditions and legal principles of which it is part and their current uses and applications. The aim is for halal registered enterprises and their personnel to understand and appreciate the concept of halal in terms of the norms and standards it embodies and the moral basis of its compliance requirements. The essay explains halal and associated concepts by reference to the original Quranic sources and links them with current compliance standards of the major halal importers like Indonesia and the UAE. It also discusses both the weaknesses of the current halal certification system operating in Australia, and elsewhere in the western world in the context of halal development. Together with the article on "Halal development: Beyond the Rubber Stamp Syndrome", it conceives of halal producers and other halal stakeholders as active participants in and members of a broad community of interests called the halal community.

The idea of a halal community is given specificity in the latter essay (chapter 6). That essay is a pointed critique of the halal certification system, particularly the way it is applied by current halal certifiers as it is about the need for halal development. It looks at the standard of certification services they offer to business and finds them to be poor and inadequate- with excessive reliance by some on the rubberstamp as the primary tool and others using it as the only tool of halal certification. It argues that the weaknesses of halal certification organisations (which claim to be but in many cases are not Islamic societies) stem largely from the model on which they are built and the structures that they operate. It calls for a major reform to develop the field of halal trade and commerce and to strengthen its universal credentials by creating a new model of halal certification organisations better suited to a modern, complex and global business landscape. It proposes an alternative model and offers suggestions how it might be constructed. Chapter 7 is an inspection report of a halal establishment. The inspection, which I have conducted, finds that it does not comply with halal standards despite the fact that it is a halal registered establishment supervised by both a government supervisor and a halal certification organisation. It represents a failure of halal control and is a graphic illustration of how not to operate a halal establishment.

Chapter 8 is submission I have written to the Senate inquiry into Animal Welfare Standards in Australia's Livestock Exports with specific reference to live cattle exports to Indonesia. The inquiry was brought about by the public outcry following the screening on the Australian Broadcasting Corporation (ABC) Four corners Program on 31 May 2011, of a footage showing graphic images of cruelty to Australian cattle exports in Indonesian abattoirs. The emphasis of the submission is how to find an appropriate and effective solution to this persistent problem not only in Indonesia but in other export destinations- particularly Muslim countries. Very minor changes have been made to the submission.

Australia is a major player in the global halal market and therefore has a big stake in its economic health as well as in its development. The market is no longer limited to Muslim and Muslim majority countries. In fact it always had a global foundation and reference. There is a vague recognition of this in the making of both the Brunei global halal brand and the MLA global halal brand. The halal market is experiencing significant expansion and growth and with it the emergence of hitherto unidentified and unrecognised categories of halal consumers. It is a trend which is likely to continue and grow stronger. That growth is evident in Australia. Some enterprises have been successful in making their products universally halal by adopting the halal method, without compromising their traditional customers. A good example is the way halal registered abattoirs produce the same product for both Australian supermarkets as well as for halal export. One of the aims of this book is to alert business to these trends so that they can firstly understand and appreciate the potential of halal trade and commerce and secondly be able to respond to the opportunities which the global halal market offers. If this book stimulates interest of some business enterprises to participate or actually helps them improve their participation in the global or domestic halal market then it would have indeed served a very useful purpose. It would serve as good or even better purpose if in response to the issues raised in this book halal authorities placed halal reform and development on their agenda as a matter of high priority… and acted on it expeditiously. Furthermore if this book encourages some tertiary educational institutions to include halal and associated concepts in the studies they offer on subjects relevant to Islamic thought and practice, then it would have exceeded my expectations.

There is an ongoing debate about halal development in which issues such as halal management, halal standards, transparency and professionalism are central. This book is a contribution to that debate.

Chapter 1

Producing Halal Food: Why, How and for Whom?

Introduction

A proactive and targeted strategy would enable enterprises that produce or want to produce halal goods and services to capture a significantly larger share of the global halal market of 1.7 billion consumers than they currently do. This chapter explains the principles, rules and procedures required for halal food exports to Muslim and Muslim majority countries as well as to the global halal market.

Halal Food and Commercial Interests

Halal food is a fast growing area of commerce. Countries such as Australia and New Zealand are becoming some of the major exporters of Halal meat in the world. The rules regarding halal production and consumption are enshrined in Islamic law (the *Sharia*). Islam is a primary source of identity for 1.7 billion people around the world, which is estimated to be a quarter of the world's population (Pew Research centre 2011). Some of Australia's closest neighbours such as Indonesia and Malaysia are Muslim or Muslim majority countries. They require their food imports to comply with *Sharia* based halal standards. According to a study conducted by the pew research Centre in 2010 and released in January 2011 Indonesia has the largest Muslim population in the world which accounts for 88 percent of its own population and 80 percent of all Muslims living in South East Asia (Pew Research Centre 2011).

In these and other Muslim countries in the Middle East, many western countries have considerable commercial, political and strategic interests. Their demand for halal food is huge and increasing rapidly. Some of the Gulf Cooperation Council countries- comprising Saudi Arabia, United Arab Emirates, Oman, Kuwait, Qatar and Bahrain- have high per capita incomes, the fastest growing middle classes and one the highest birth rates in the world. They import almost all their food needs and are interested in investing in agriculture in countries that can provide food security for their populations.

For Muslims Islam is not just a religion. It is also importantly a cultural commitment and a way of life. It permeates their habits, their expectations, their work practices, their communication patterns, the organisation of their time as well as their business and social relations. The conception of religion is not limited to a narrow sphere of human existence but is broad and comprehensive in the scope and extent of its coverage. Markets are part of that comprehensive outlook of human existence. They do not occupy a separate and unrelated domain. Rather, they are inextricably linked to religious values and on account of this can be characterised as being halal markets or having certain halal characteristics in order to distinguish them from others that are not halal or do not have those characteristics.

Muslim Law and Doctrine

The Quran, the Holy Book of Islam, and the *Sunna*, Prophet Mohammed's traditions, constitute the twin sources of Islamic doctrine and law including religious and moral guidance.

Central to Muslim law and doctrine are the concepts of halal and haram. They are composite principles which address both the spiritual and material concerns of mankind. They constitute the practical application of the Islamic belief system, giving expression to core cultural and moral imperatives, which regulate daily human existence, behaviour and conduct. The term halal means that which is permitted and therefore lawful in Islam. Conversely haram is that which is prohibited or is unlawful. In this article we are not concerned with halal and haram in their broadest scope but only in so far as they relate to the production, manufacture and export of food.

Halal as a Universal Standard

The halal requirement in Islam signifies the adoption of a standard system of rules and practices in, for example, the production, manufacture, processing, transportation, storage and sale of food and beverages, which can be validated as having a halal status. In non-Muslim countries, the fulfillment of these requirements by way of monitoring and certification by a recognised halal authority sanctions the handling of and trading in that product and its consumption by Muslims throughout the world.

What is most striking about the halal system, as a whole, is firstly its simplicity and secondly the high degree of uniformity of its standard requirements across the world. In view of this, it can be appropriately identified as a single and separate food market. In terms of its scope and potential it is the single largest food market in the world. The significance of this proposition is all the more compelling in view of the fact that the halal system applies to business, finance and investment products and services as it does to Halal food.

Acceptance of this view would necessitate a radical shift in the way Australia and other major Halal exporters conduct this trade, a shift of such magnitude that it might present a serious challenge to conventional policy assumptions and strategic thinking. Neither Australian governments nor halal food exporters nor industry organisations are attuned to this view, despite compelling reasons that they should be. Instead of comprehending halal as a universal system, as Muslims comprehend it, there is a widespread and persisting tendency to see it purely in terms of multifarious product specifications. This mistaken view may be partly responsible why there has been little effort in taking advantage of the immense opportunities that the global Halal market offers. Lack of sufficient appreciation of halal is also a major factor in the Australian government's failure to resolve the recurrent animal welfare problems associated with its livestock exports to Indonesia and other Muslim countries which has persisted for the past twenty years.

Basic Halal Rules

It is relatively simple to produce, manufacture and export halal food and beverages. In Islam, the scope of food which is halal is almost unlimited. Emphasising God's bounty and blessing, everything is permitted for human consumption, benefit and use except for a very few items, specifically forbidden as haram by an explicit Quranic injunction or authentic *Sunna* (tradition) of the Prophet Mohammed. There are only six categories of food and beverages which are prohibited (Al Quran 5:3; 5:4):

1. Flesh of dead animals or carrion; that which has been killed by strangling, by beating, by falling or by being gored or its head crushed, and that which has been eaten by a wild beast
2. Swine and all products and ingredients containing or derived from it
3. Flowing or congealed blood
4. Intoxicants – alcohol and drugs
5. Immolated / sacrificed unto false idols
6. Carnivorous animals with fangs or birds of prey with sharp claws

The first five are explicitly stated in the *Quran*; the last is based on the *Sunna*.

In Muslim belief, the justifications of Islam's prohibition or haram are by no means arbitrary or purely transcendental. Rather they are based on considerations of human welfare and for the good of mankind; hence the conception of halal as that which is wholesome, good and beneficial for human beings (Al-Qaradawi undated). Perhaps no other example illustrates more clearly the justifications for prohibition of certain products than alcohol (and by extension other intoxicants). While acknowledging its benefit, the Quran states categorically that its harm to human beings far outweighs any benefit it has and it is for that reason haram (prohibited).

> They ask thee concerning wine [alcohol & drugs] and gambling.
>
> Say: In them there is great harm and some benefit for human beings, but the harm is far greater than the benefit (Al Quran 2:219).

Where the law is completely silent, and no inference can be drawn whatsoever on its position, then that product or activity is halal (permitted) and should under no circumstances by included in the haram or prohibited category (Al Qaradawi undated).

Increasing Demand for Halal Food and Beverages

Muslim and Muslim majority countries (including Muslim minority countries like Singapore) are increasingly insisting on halal certified products to satisfy the demands of Muslims consumers. To this end they have developed country specific regulations and orders based on the Islamic *Sharia* to control the importation of halal food and beverages. There is likelihood, given pressures on governments that some countries may extend this control to cosmetics, with a possibility of expanding it to some pharmaceutical products. Overtime there will be a much wider range and volume of products that will require halal certification and compliance with *Sharia* based halal standards. While many of the reports on the halal market focus on meat, the halal label covers every agri-food product from cereals, sauces ice cream, to bottled water (see Agriculture and Agri-Food Canada 2007).

In Australia, where the Muslim population is more than 400,000, many halal products are appearing on supermarket shelves. In the last fifteen years the number specialised halal restaurants, grocery stores, butchers and other food shops has increased dramatically in major cities, no doubt stimulated to a considerable extent by the international trade in halal food. In western countries and internationally halal food consumption is not limited to Muslims. Rapidly Increasing numbers of non-Muslims are also consuming halal products in greater and greater quantities. According to the Agriculture and Agri-Food Canada, "... consumers are seeking halal food due to halal food's excellent reputation for healthy and safe food products, and the humane treatment of animals", (2011). These may not be all the real reasons or indeed the only ones why demand for halal remains strong. Moreover, while it is reasonable to say that halal reputation is good, the attribution of excellence regarding its practice to the degree that is claimed above is no doubt exaggerated (see chapter 2). The halal system has a long way to go in its development to achieve the level of excellence required by its (Quranic) foundational tenets.

The question of product labelling, more precisely of false, misleading and inaccurate labelling, of packaged foods has become a major concern for many halal importing countries. The problems associated with labelling are not limited to product content but extend to the authenticity of the halal claims expressed on the logo and other inscriptions used on the product label as well as the authority and status of its certifier (Al Katheeri 1996). In response to this concern, some countries such as the Gulf Cooperation Council (GCC), a regional body consisting of Bahrain, Kuwait, Oman, Qatar, Saudi Arabia and the United Arab Emirates (UAE) have developed and are now applying more stringent standards for labelling than had hitherto been the case (SMO for GCC 1984).

In Muslim and Muslim majority countries, the central control structure of halal food and beverages importation consists of two separate institutions working in close cooperation. They are the halal authority and the Department of Veterinary Services. This seems to be the most commonly used model for halal control. Officials from these institutions (in Malaysia, Indonesia and UAE) visit non-Muslim exporting countries such as Australia from time to time, for audit and evaluation purposes and for the inspection of those establishments operating under a halal program. In Malaysia, the halal authority is part of the Department of the Prime Minister, which is indicative of the importance the government attaches to this field of commerce. In Indonesia it is the peak religious body namely Majelis Ulama Indonesia or MUIS.

Accreditation of Halal Food Agencies in Australia

The halal authorities in these countries are represented in halal exporting non-Muslim countries like Australia by local Islamic organisations, which are accredited/ listed as agents to supervise, monitor and certify halal food exports. In order for a local Islamic organisation to be accredited / listed as a halal export certifier and services provider, it must apply for official approval from each Muslim country it wishes to represent. A list of the local accredited organisations and the Muslim countries they represent can be obtained from Aus-Meat or the Australian Quarantine and Inspection Service (AQIS). Any country may withdraw its accreditation/ listing, if it believes that an accredited organisation has failed to fulfill its responsibilities as a halal certifying and monitoring organisation.

There are approximately 13 accredited organisations in Australia, ranging from those that represent one or two countries to those that represent the majority of halal importing countries; some are well known internationally, others are not so well known (see appendix 6 for list of accredited halal certifiers in 2010). There are only four major ones. They vary to a greater or lesser degree in their capabilities with regard to the provision of halal services. Their halal management structures also differ in form with some operating as Mosque establishments and others as specialised halal service organisations.

Any halal exporter, manufacturer or abattoir can choose from these organisations, the one which is most competent to provide it with its halal service needs. In making this choice, it is not necessarily the case that the certifier that the exporter finds easiest to deal with is the most competent, the most widely respected or recognised. It is highly likely that the certifier who is more stringent in the application of halal rules and procedural requirements better serves the interests of the exporter and the industry as a whole. The halal food regulatory requirements as well as the procedures for the production, processing, supervision and certification of halal food exports presented here are based primarily on the system applied by the Islamic Coordinating Council of Australia (ICCA 1997) in Melbourne. Key provisions of other major organisations are incorporated in order to present a composite picture.

Certifying a product as halal by ICCA and similar agencies means a seal of approval that it is properly supervised and has met all the halal status requirements through all stages of production, processing, transportation and storage. What this certification does in effect is to engender confidence in consumers in importing countries as to the authenticity of the product as halal. In that sense also it is a powerful promotional tool for that product to attract halal customers.

Basic conditions of Halal Slaughter

In Islam, the killing of animals is solely for human sustenance. It must therefore be done in way that causes least pain within a prescribed method as follows:

- The name of God must be invoked while slaughtering by blessing it and saying: Bismillah, Allahu Akbar (In the name of God; God is Great)
- The animal must be slaughtered (its throat cut) with a sharp object in one swift and uninterrupted movement, which is capable of making it bleed by severing the blood vessels
- At no time must the knife by lifted while slaughtering. The slaughter must be in such a way that the respiratory and jugular veins are quickly cut. The head is to remain on the dead animal until dressing starts
- The slaughterman must be a practicing Muslim.

Halal Requirements for Abattoirs

1. All slaughtermen must be approved by ICCA or similarly accredited agencies and registered with AQIS
2. All slaughtermen must be registered with Aus-Meat and carry their identity cards at all times
3. Pig meat must not be slaughtered, processed or stored in the abattoir
4. Stunning may be carried out prior to slaughter so long as the animal's heart continues to beat after stunning. It is necessary that all animals

receive a head-only stun. The animal must be able to regain consciousness if need be before the halal cut is made. Stunning parameters should be as follows: between 0.5 and 0.9 amps for three seconds and with the halal cut to be made within six seconds of stunning.

5. Processing of the carcasses must not commence until the animal is completely dead. This is approximately 3-4 minutes after slaughter.
6. All carcasses must be clearly identified with an official VIC MS stamp in the case of Victoria, or the relevant MS stamp in other states.
7. Non-halal carcasses shall be stored in separate chiller or on separate rails with at least one clear rail between halal slaughtered and non-halal slaughtered carcasses.
8. Offal from non-halal carcasses shall be packed separately from halal products, prepared a viscera table and placed in containers labeled non-halal. The non-halal product shall be periodically removed from the room by the Muslim supervisor. Where a non-halal product is packed prior to ta halal product, the offal room shall be completely cleaned before the commencement of the halal product.
9. In the boning room, halal carcasses shall be boned out separately from non-halal carcasses. Prior to the commencement of halal boning operations, all non-halal meat will be packed and cleared from the boning room. This will be followed by dry clean up of the room, complete wash down of all meat packing and slicing tables and knives and change of all cutting boards.
10. The halal product, once cartoned, shall be stamped halal, conveyed to the blast chiller or transported to a halal registered cold storage for freezing. Halal cartoned products shall be palletized and stacked separately from non-halal products in the blast chiller and during transit to and storage at cold stores.
11. The halal product shall be transported on separate racks or pallets or on a separate truck. It shall be identified by a clear halal impression of a halal brand.
12. A transfer certificate must accompany every halal load transported from the abattoir to the boning room or cold store.
13. All halal products loaded out from the abattoir for export must be accompanied by a halal interim certificate.

14. A Muslim inspector in the abattoir is responsible for all halal activities including supervision of loading out and issuing transfer and interim certificates.

Halal Requirements for Boning Rooms

The same conditions which apply to abattoirs also apply to boning establishments, with respect to segregation of halal from non-halal, cleaning, certification, packing and impressing cartoned products with a halal stamp and a relevant MS stamp. It is imperative that all halal products coming into the boning room from other establishments are accompanied by a halal transfer certificate and received by a Muslim inspector.

Halal Requirements for Cold Stores

1. All incoming halal loads must be received by a Muslim inspector.
2. Halal products must be separately stored during blast freezing.
3. Frozen halal products must remain isolated from non-halal products in the freezer.
4. Halal products shall be loaded out separately from non-halal products under the supervision of a Muslim inspector
5. All halal products transported out from the cold store must be accompanied by a transfer certificate
6. All halal products loaded for export must be accompanied by a halal interim certificate
7. An official *'Certificate for Meat Slaughtered by Muslims'* signed by ICCA or the relevant Islamic Society and AQIS must accompany halal products to their export destinations. Without this certificate products may be deemed non-halal by importing countries.

Applying for Halal Approval - Mainly Processed Food

1. The first step for a business to apply for Halal approval for a product is to complete a Company Profile Form. Along with this form the applicant should complete and submit a form entitled Halal Product Submission Form to ICCA where both forms are available. A halal Product Submission Form must be completed for each product seeking halal approval.
2. Each halal Product Submission Form must be accompanied by related ingredients data sheet. A technical specification sheet is required for every ingredient used in the manufacture of the product in question.
3. Once the application is received by ICCA, it is submitted to a technical evaluation team to consider the halal status of the ingredients. If any of the ingredients conflict with the halal requirements, then the product is rejected and shall not obtain halal approval. If on the other hand, it conforms with these requirements, then the investigation proceeds as outlined below.
4. The applicant has the option of terminating the investigation into the product which has been rejected or alternatively may choose to find a replacement or substitute ingredient which complies with halal requirements.
5. Once the technical evaluation team has finalised its investigation, a physical inspection of the plant is carried out by ICCA.
6. After performing the plant inspection and being satisfied that the product conforms with the guidelines and requirements of halal production, ICCA grants halal approval to the product. This is done firstly by signing a contract between the applicant and ICCA and secondly, by issuing the applicant with a Halal Certificate for the product. There are also a number of other related terms and conditions to be discussed.

Conclusion

It would be misleading to interpret the regulatory and procedural requirements of halal food presented in this paper as being difficult to meet. In fact they are no more difficult, once properly understood, nor arguably in effect more costly, than for comparable non-halal products.

Compelling evidence of how easy it is to adopt the halal system is the number of halal registered establishments in Australia. According to Aus-Meat (1999) there were 97 Malaysian listed slaughtering, meat processing and boning rooms operating export halal programs. Every year there are more coming onto and registering for the halal program. They are doing so on no other grounds than economic considerations with the relative cost and benefit of the alternative as the paramount consideration. Allegro, a family owned export Meat Company based in Western Australia states that 'halal meat is a specialty of Allegro Pty Ltd; 90% of its $90 million per annum turnover is generated by the sale of meat products derived from Animals slaughtered to Islamic rites'.

It is on these grounds that Bonlac Foods Australia's largest dairy company, has chosen to produce all its products under the halal system (Giles 1996). Many abattoirs and boning rooms have taken the same course.

Chapter 2

Responding to Consumer and Industry Trends through Halal Certification

Introduction

Halal consumers are a relatively new category of consumers in the markets of western countries. They have rarely been given attention by writers in the literature of social sciences including economics and marketing. This paper explores the dynamic relationship between this category of consumers and producers of halal goods and services from the perspective of western enterprises. It shows how that relationship is changing and how it can with the proper strategy and approach bring about an unprecedented expansion of consumers globally and consequently of sales outcomes. It challenges the concept of halal consumers as it is commonly understood and posits an alternative more accurate apprehension of who they are. In the process it identifies and brings to the fore sub-categories of halal consumers that had been hitherto unacknowledged and unrecognized. The key strategy in achieving a global expansion of halal customers, it is posited is through halal certification. The paper explains how halal certification if adopted by producers can attract sub-categories of consumers that are likely to significantly increase the growth in the number of consumers willing to buy the firms' products in the marketplace.

The Relationship: Consumers and Enterprises that Produce Goods and Services

The first part of the topic presumes an existing and necessary relationship between consumers and Industry- or business enterprises. That it is a necessary relationship is a concrete reality grounded in social and economic interaction and exchange. Firms produce goods and services for no apparent reason other than to satisfy the wants of consumers, whoever they might be, and to profit form it. Consumers not only expect enterprises to produce the goods and services they want; they also exercise choice in purchasing one product in preference to another. They do so by buying more in quantity of a particular product than another, or none of it at all. In this way, consumers determine what goods and services enterprises produce to satisfy their wants. The centre of this exchange is of course the marketplace- a complex, dynamic and diverse places where choices are expressed in ways that are determinative and consequential for enterprises that produce the goods and services in any given marketplace. In turn this enables enterprises to satisfy the wants of consumers in the quantities they want at the prices different categories of consumers can afford. The enterprises' profitability and their survival depend on decisions and choices consumers make everyday.

The Consumer as Sovereign

This is a very general presentation of the relationship of consumers and enterprises, found in text books in marketing, economic and commerce. They show the centrality of the consumer choice in the production of goods and services in the market economy, where sometimes the consumer is charcterised as King or Sovereign. In modern economies the consumer is in sometimes characterised as an ideal, all too powerful sovereign but in reality he is far less so as he can be a guided, managed and manipulated, as many influences work on him/her through the subtle and subliminal images of advertising and marketing. Given the overwhelming impacts of these influences some may be inclined to see him/her more of a slave than king or queen. In order to attract him, he is subjected to a bewildering array of powerful images that guide his orientation and create and raise his desire to buy, and buy more of particular products than others. Images are for example utilised to appeal to his culture, values, class etc. and among a range other personal characteristics to his vanity, prejudices, inclination and proclivities. An important aspect of this is the creation of a persona that enables him to identify with and be loyal to the products he purchases and through this have an affinity with global consumers of the same or similar products and services- expressed in brand loyalty. Through this construction his identity is constituted and given specificity. Thus his comfort zone is created and his level of satisfaction is raised to a higher plane than hitherto. Despite these influences and pressures the decisions he/she makes determines what enterprises produce, how they produce them and in what quantities. The challenge of enterprises is not only to understand how he makes his choices but more importantly how to influence them.

Influences on the Halal Consumer

The Muslim halal consumer is not immune from these pressures. His comfort zone and the bedrock of his orientation and values embodied in that comfort zone are however markedly different. What distinguishes him from other consumers is his loyalty and commitment to halal over all other loyalties. It is the litmus test by means of which he determines whether he buys a particular product or not. Thus, in the first instance his/her world is a halal world and his decisions are made through or mediated by the prism of whether a product is halal or haram. That halal world is by no means an exclusive one, but is one in which halal is paramount such that it mediates production, consumption, and sale of goods and services. Of course he/she proceeds from the position, the knowledge and certainty that the overwhelming majority of goods that are grown or produced naturally are generically or in origin (*Asl*) halal and that by comparison a small number are haram or prohibited in Islam (Al Qardawi undated). In choosing these generic halal products that need no halal validation or approval, he shares the same skewed responses, exhibits the same predilections, and is acted upon by the same influences as his non-halal consuming counterparts. Though by comparison small however, in the range of products and in absolute numbers, the goods and services that need halal approval or compliance are huge and growing fast. Further still halal consumers generally have by training, outlook and socialisation a healthy skepticism, or suspicion about many products that claim to be generically halal and even those that claim to have a halal status and may even be halal compliant. Where suspicion or doubt is strong, prohibition is not explicitly imposed, but Islam enjoins its adherents to avoid such products and services, lest they be haram, or contain haram constituents in some proportion or another (Al Qardawi undated). Muslims generally see this as being tantamount to prohibition. Enterprises must be aware of and be able to negotiate these matters at the coalface. Legitimate halal certification is the quintessential tool to dispel any doubts Muslim consumers may have about halal products and services.

The Importance of Halal Consumers and the Halal Trade

Why then should we be concerned with halal and why should attention to it be warranted? From a purely economic perspective, the first and simplest answer is this: if we accept the central position consumers have in the operation of the market, then there are over 1.7 billion Muslim consumers in the world that want to buy halal goods and services. That is a massive number of people by any measure- representing about a quarter of the world's population. A growing number of non-Muslim consumers are also buying halal products. According to the Pew Research Centre's projections, the global Muslim population is expected to increase by about 35 per cent rising from 1.6 billion in 2010 to 2.2 billion in 2030. A prominent feature of this growth is that it shall be twice the rate of growth of the non-Muslim population over the next two decades. " If the current trend continues Muslims will make up 26.4 per cent of the world's total projected population of 8.3 billion in 2030, up from 23.4 per cent of the estimated 2010 world population of 6.9 billion" (Pew Research Center : 2011).

According to the Agriculture and Agri.-Food Canada, the global Halal food market is on the threshold of major developments that hold the promise of rapid and sustained growth (2007). It states that in 2010 it accounted for as much as 17 per cent of the global trade in agri-food products and forecasts that major growth will generate growth opportunities throughout the agri-food industry (Agriculture and Agri-Food Canada 2011). Much higher yearly growth projections of 20 to 30 per cent are claimed by at least one other source (See Soesilwati 2010). The global market for halal food alone is estimated to be more than $580 billion annually (Hamid: 2008; Soesilwati: 2010)). There are similar but higher estimates. According to Agri-Food Canada it was valued in 2010 at US$661 billion, a figure sourced from the World Halal Forum table below (2011).

Table 1 Global Halal Food Market Size by Region (US$)

Region/Year	2009	2010	% change
Africa	150.6 billion	155.9 billion	3.50%
Asia	400.0 billion	418.1 billion	4.50%
Europe	66.6 billion	69.3 billion	4.10%
Australia/ Oceania	1.2 billion	1.6 billion	33.30%
Americas	16.1 billion	16.7 billion	3.60%
Total Halal Food Market Size	634.5 billion	661.6 billion	4.30%

Source: World Halal Forum 2009 Post Event Report and the 6th World Halal Forum Presentation

If non-food halal products are included (such as cosmetics, personal care products and pharmaceuticals etc.) then the value of the market is estimated to be more than $ 2 trillion annually. In addition "the present trend in consumer demand for halal products is expected to continue, in tandem with increasing size of the Muslim population" (Halal Research Council 2006). Except for these estimates, there are no reliable statistics on the value of global halal market. But even allowing for a reasonable margin of error they show the huge opportunities in halal trade and commerce. There is no doubt that the halal trade is substantial both in volume and value, nor is there doubt that the halal market is one of the biggest food importing markets in the world. Many reports on the halal market focus on meat, but products sold under the halal label cover virtually every agri-product plus non-food products such as cosmetics (Food and Agri-Food Canada 2007). From a religious and moral perspective, it is not simply that Muslims have a preference for or just an inclination or desire to buy halal. Rather it is that Islam enjoins its adherents to consume that which is halal, defined as that which is wholesome, good and beneficial for mankind and to abstain from that which is haram or prohibited and by definition harmful to humans (Al Qardawi undated). Halal is for Muslims both a religious moral imperative and fundamental expression of one's identity.

Beyond its immediate benefits, no other area of trade has the capacity to offer greater opportunities for engagement with the Muslim world on so many other fronts than halal trade and commerce. That it can do so demonstrates the overwhelming impact of culture and particularly religious morality and how it generally dominates Muslim behavior and conduct. If carefully planned it can open up many avenues for it to be utilised effectively as an instrument to support, deepen and entrench wider and related commercial, political and strategic interests. More than any other instrument it makes these engagements meaningful, productive and purposeful. It makes explicit how culture is a dominant influence on Muslim societies and how it underpins and shapes key decisions and patterns decision making processes. While it is most manifest in the production, consumption and sale of halal goods and services its overall influence in other areas is nonetheless real and no less formidable. Much more than simply applying it to production techniques of commercial enterprises as regulatory framework, it is fundamentally a world view that conditions how Muslims think about the world and act in it, including how they conduct commercial operations and what they aim to achieve by it.

The more western enterprises and other institutions ignore its influence the weaker their impact is likely to be in the marketplace and the decisions that inform it. What this tells us is that for western enterprises to engage productively there should be a paradigm shift in how they do business with the Muslim world in order to maximise business opportunities. This is not to deny that trade with the Muslim world is strong, but to assert that it is far below the capacity of what it could be, and much less productive than if the concept was applied strategically in support of trade and commerce. To chart out a new course then, the task of trading with and producing for this market needs to be differently conceived and practised than has been the case in the past. Among the questions that enterprises need to ask themselves is: how can we best produce for this market? How do we conceive and apprehend Halal consumers? What methods are necessary to satisfy their needs? And how can we best engage them in order to have a mutually beneficial relationship with them? In any response it would be difficult to avoid halal values in mediating the process of adaptation to the marketplace and bringing them to bear upon the common interest involved in the project of trading.

Underlying Barriers to Halal Trade

The huge capacity of Muslims for and commitment to the consumption of halal goods and services has not been totally ignored by western enterprises. Most importantly however it has not been sufficiently appreciated by them. This is neither solely due to the lack of understanding by western enterprises of what halal is or how the system works in practice, nor for that matter to resistance, on their part to adopt or accommodate it. Nevertheless it is true to say that some halal establishments have utilised it well technically without necessarily recognising its global potential or the values underpinning it. Others struggle to adjust to its standards yet persist by making short cuts to meet them. Meat and livestock Australia has for example created a halal brand for itself that appears not to conform with halal norms. These are no doubt all factors that to a greater or lesser extent explain why the adoption by enterprises of the halal standard has been very slow on the uptake. That they are however distinguished by being enterprise-related factors are in themselves significant in so far as they indicate where possible improvements can be made and appropriate solutions can be sought. No doubt there are also real difficulties enterprises face in adopting halal which are outside their control. There is certainly need for greater willingness to apprehend halal on its own terms and to appreciate that its foundations are built on religious moral imperatives that are at once universal and permanent from an Islamic perspective. They are however only part of a more complex equation.

The other, more fundamental side of that equation is that which pertains to halal organisations, structures, systems and their capabilities. The problems associated with these are deeper and may have more direct adverse affects on the pace of development, growth, as well as the speed of adaptation by western enterprises to the halal system. As it currently operates, the halal standard and the systems that operationalise it can appear to be somewhat confusing if not at times contradictory. There is sufficient evidence to suggest that both in terms of professional competence and in terms of operational structures most halal certifiers are ill-equipped to cater adequately for the complex needs of modern business. To some Muslim observers, there is an apparent mismatch between the foundational claims of halal and its operation on the ground. Its inherent universality and uniformity as a standard is for example strikingly contradicted by the diversity of its application. On the whole it does not inspire confidence nor provide encouragement to enterprises to embrace it as their preferred method of operation, even though a growing number have done so on considerations of its market potential rather than on its merits. That it has been slow on the uptake is therefore not at all surprising. Nor is it surprising in view of the above considerations that, Muslim consumers generally and halal authorities in particular have been slow in communicating their halal needs and have been unable to present a uniform standard for enterprises to follow and gain access to halal markets worldwide. The failure on the part of enterprises is that they have not been proactive or particularly keen to learn about halal and to respond boldly with ingenuity to the huge demand the global halal market offers for no other motive than that of their own self interest. At present commercial halal requirements are relevant to and can be broadly applied to the following goods and services:

- Food and beverages
- Pharmaceutical products and health care products
- Cosmetics & personal care products
- Banking and other financial services
- Branding, marketing and promotion
- Charitable and disaster relief products & services

Emergence of Halal Food Products in Western Markets

The Muslim world has generally experienced a rapid economic and social development in the last fifty years. In some countries development has been swift and no less remarkable. With this development came a huge appetite for consumption of all kinds of goods and services. The strongest growth in consumption occurred in wealthy oil producing states of the Middle East and North Africa-almost all of it from western countries for modernisation. Buttressed by oil wealth the sharp increase in consumption was underpinned by a number of factors including strong growth in disposable incomes and equally strong growth in youth population and educational advancement. The growth in the demand for halal products, particularly meat, and their importation from western countries followed this period. It has been stimulated in part by the settlement of many Muslims in the West during this period. The liberalisation of trade and the development of modern communications provided further impetus and enabled western firms to respond to Muslim consumer demand for products including halal more quickly than in the past. Still halal consumer demand remained for a long time obscure and awareness of it uneven and superficial. To be sure halal consumers are not a new category of consumers that burst into the marketplace only with advent of oil ascendancy. Rather they are a well defined category of consumers distinguished by having a distinct identity, culture and values grounded in Islamic history and society. Certification accompanied these developments and was a consequence of the demand by halal consumers for halal compliant food products from western firms. There were also parallel developments in demand by halal consumers for halal (or Islamic) banking and financial products, but this remained local to Muslim countries and presented a strong and viable competition to non-Islamic banking- or more appropriately non-halal banking. Since the 2008 global financial crisis there has been unprecedented interest in Islamic banking principles due to, among other things, their apparent financial stability, "interest-free loans" and lower exposure to risk compared to major western banks.

Halal Certification: Focus and Definition

This brings us to the second part of this topic which sets the context of our presentation. It directs us to explore not simply the relationship between enterprises and consumers but how the former can respond to a specific type of consumer. In effect it identifies for us, albeit indirectly though unambiguously, who that consumer is and in doing so points to the kind of products and service he is likely to purchase. Hence the question how can enterprises satisfy his wants and provide him with the kind of products he is likely to buy? The key to the satisfaction of his wants is not so much the characteristics of the product or its general appeal, important though these are, but rather the values and ethic it embodies, the identity it claims to have and ultimately the validation of such claims in the marketplace. Without these necessary attributes the likelihood is that he/she will not purchase it, if it is within scope of products that require halal validation- and particularly if it is a meat product. Validation in this context is by way of a certification process and not any kind of certification but specifically halal certification. The specificity of this reference is significant in that it identifies for us the type of consumers to which the first part of the question refers. By the same token halal certification can only refer to halal consumers, without which halal certification would not apply. By applying the instrument and ethic of halal certification the aim is to satisfy a category of consumers called or characterized as halal consumers. The topic therefore invites us to explore specific related categories in the economic cycle: halal consumers, firms that want to produce halal goods and services and the rules, processes and values that underpin their production and sale- halal certification. This relationship is a unique and contingent one in the sense that it cannot operate satisfactorily without halal certification and if it were made to do so it would be found to be deficient and in most circumstances invalid. In other words the absence of halal certification is highly likely to render the goods and services produced by the firm unfit for consumption by Muslim halal consumers. The relationship expressed in this way pertains to products requiring halal status. How strong or weak that relationship is for a particular enterprise at any given time can be represented by the following two diagrams.

Figures 1&2 weak and strong halal certification

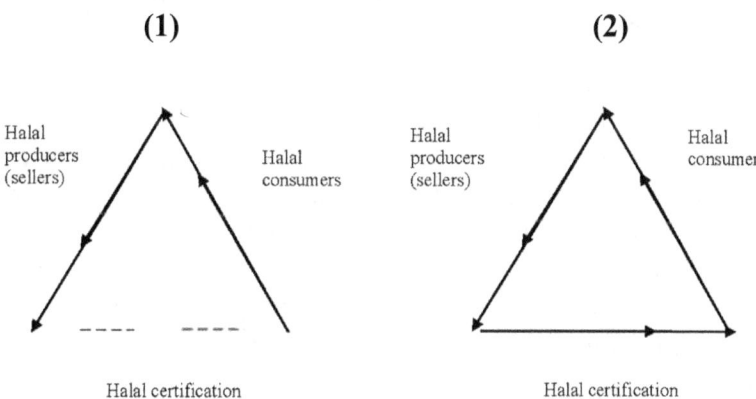

Together the two diagrams show that the relationship can not occur without it being mediated by halal certification, with figure (1) representing a weak and unreliable certification and figure (2) representing a strong and reliable & in this case perfect halal certification. In figure (1) the broken lines represent weaknesses in the system of certification. The interruptions in the flow of the line and therefore in the relationship occurs because certification system is not sufficiently developed, fully reliable or credible and may be deficient in aspects of its operation for the halal consumer to have full confidence in it. Hence the weakness in certification gives rise to corresponding broken lines representing a broken pattern in the halal consumers' willingness to purchase products because of uncertainty about or lack of confidence in halal certification. The bigger the gaps between the broken lines are, the weaker the relationship between halal consumers on the one hand and halal producers and sellers on the other. In the extreme the complete absence of a connecting certification line(s) means the complete absence of any relationship between them. Some of the reasons that give rise to the weaknesses in certification may be as follows:

- Absence of or concern about halal certification
- Lack of uniformity, consistency and credibility in certification
- Lack of confidence in a certifier or in his authority to certify
- Inconsistent and/or poor standard of service provision by certifier
- Competition with unapproved halal certification or halal logos
- Serious doubt about the authenticity of certification and hence about the halal status of products produced under this certification regime

In contrast with the weaknesses in certification and their negative impact represented by the broken line in figure (1), figure (2) shows a firm unbroken line representing the (ideal) positive role and impact of halal certification on the relationship between halal consumers and halal producers. In this relationship, the less broken the line, the less interruption in the flow of relationship is between the two. With the improvement and development of the halal certification system over time the broken lines will tend to disappear as they are removed by improvements that have taken place. Instead they will be replaced by smooth uninterrupted line as shown in figure (2). The unbroken line shows that there is now an uninterrupted flow of halal goods and services being purchased by halal consumers, facilitated by an efficient, strong and reliable halal certification system. This means that consumers have a very high degree, if not an absolute, confidence in the products represented in this diagram.

Before we discuss certification at greater length, first we need to say a number of important things about it. A definition to start with: Halal certification is the process by which goods and services produced by firms are issued approved halal certificate(s) by a competent authority or its representative validating them as being halal or having halal status and confirming that they have complied with an approved *Sharia* halal standard or regulations based on it. Validation or authentication is performed by way of supervision and monitoring of the production and processing of goods and services according to a recognised and approved halal standard culminating in the issuance of a certificate of authentication declaring them as halal. The document or certificate so produced accompanies the product, in the case of physical products to their export destination or local sales outlet, where further processes to maintain the integrity of the halal product may or may not be required to take place. In packaged products, in addition to certification (i.e. the provision an actual certificate), companies may use their certifying entity's logo or label on each product package. Companies use the logo in part this way as confirmation or validation instrument of halal status and secondly as a promotional tool displaying its identity and increasing the appeal and attraction of the products to halal customers. The advantage of this form of certification by itself is the immediacy of its recognition as well as its positive impact. However, this is not necessarily always a measure of its credibility or authenticity. The primary test of both the authenticity of halal certification *per se* and its credibility is the verifiability of its processes. It cannot simply be represented by a halal rubber stamp or imprint devoid of underlying process- a common practice among many certifiers but one which is clearly in contravention of halal rules and procedural requirements.

Why is Halal Certification Necessary?

Without halal certification products would not be recognised by halal consumers as having a halal status. Most Muslims may generally presume them to be haram, of dubious status or non-halal, unless they know they are generically or in origin (*Asl*) halal and therefore do not need halal approval. Genuine halal certification is the only instrument that can give utmost confidence to halal consumers. Halal certification is therefore of critical importance for firms to enter and take advantage of the opportunities which the global halal market offers. Access to this huge and lucrative market is through certification not by way of halal production alone. Halal production and processing are the necessary conditions for entry to this market; certification is the sufficient condition and the validating instrument of the whole halal process. Unverifiable halal certification, in terms of its underlying processes, is at best of dubious status, at worst invalid and in either case unacceptable. Without proper halal certification some countries may not allow products access to their markets. They may also remove products from the market as the UAE had done on one occasion, if they are found to have improper or dubious halal certification or in the case of processed meat and juices if they are detected to contain haram ingredients or additives. On that occasion, the UAE is reported to have withdrawn all processed meat products of a particular brand from the market because of these problems (Al Katheeri 1996). At one of the earliest international halal conferences for business held in Melbourne, Australia in 1996 professor Haji Aisjah Girindra then Director of Majelis Ulama Indonesia (MUI) related an incident which demonstrates the potentially serious risks, doubts about halal status or contamination of halal by haram additives can pose for national security, for business and for the economy. She stated that:

> The incident referred to as the 'pig fat issue' sprang from reports that pig meat had been used in processing many commodities in the market. The depth of concern was such that the reports spread rapidly throughout the country, reaching even the remotest districts [causing riots]. As a result many companies suffered considerable losses. The incident demonstrated most vividly that Muslim consumers had no confidence in and were highly suspicious about the halal status of products on the market. Mindful of the social and economic implications of the 'pig fat issue' both government and specialised agencies had to act (Girindra 1996).

Apart from its value as an ethical norm, halal certification is also important for other reasons. It markedly distinguishes halal products from non-halal products and offers the halal consumer the product he/she wants to buy. Furthermore it gives him/her the confidence that it is a genuine and authentic halal product, free from non-halal or haram contamination.

In the *Sharia* (Muslim law), which is the basis of halal and haram, most of the products and services in the world are generically and in origin halal and very few of them are haram. Products that are generically or in *Asl* halal do not in principle need halal certification in their original state. Examples include honey, water, milk, grains, fruit and vegetables etc. (if they are not contaminated or otherwise rendered impure). In modern times however many of the products we consume do not remain in their natural state but are processed, reprocessed and "value added". Through processing ingredients, flavours and other additives may be added, including a wide array of chemicals which may change the character, composition, taste, smell and colour of goods for various reasons; often to appeal to the customer in one way or another, to increase the shelf life of products or as a bonding agent etc. As a result products that would otherwise remain halal generically or in origin can be and are in many cases rendered non-halal or haram. Even bottled water, for these and other reasons, can come under suspicion or raise uncertainty among halal consumers. Given his/her world being a halal world, the customer is therefore legitimately concerned if the halal status of the products he is buying have been adversely affected or contaminated by non-halal additives: hence his overwhelming reliance on halal certification.

A major consequence of modern processing of products is that it has dramatically increased the scope and number of products that require halal status. As a result, for example, a can of fruit juice or a bottle of honey or a packet of yoghurt that may have been traditionally halal is now required to be subjected to halal certification, in part because other competing products are haram or of dubious or uncertain halal status. They may also simply want to distinguish themselves from or gain advantage over other products that do not have halal certification. These examples indicate the impact modern methods of production on how halal is produced, manufactured and rendered in the marketplace. Certification is quintessential response to these developments by maintaining the integrity of halal products. In this context certification, if applied correctly, is an effective instrument and ethic:

- To clearly and unambiguously distinguish halal from haram products and services
- To underscore and highlight the identity and status of products as having halal status and being halal compliant
- To appeal to and capture the attention of halal and potential halal consumers
- To increase halal consumers awareness and confidence in the producer and the products being sold and to allay any suspicions they might otherwise have
- To enhance the reputation of a brand and the trust consumers have in the products that bear it
- To gain advantage over competing products and services

Halal Certification: A Cautionary Note

To say that halal certification is a sufficient condition for validation of halal goods and services is only true to the extent that such certification has a high degree of credibility. At one level credibility is by its very nature contestable. At another basic level credibility in this context pertains to the degree to which consumers, competent authorities and other stakeholders can have confidence in a particular certifier's endorsements of products as halal or having a halal status: in other words the adequacy and credibility of his certification process. In this sense credibility refers to the credentials, the integrity and reputation of the certifier, and his level of competence in carrying out the duties he is assigned to do both in regard to fulfilling the halal requirements of each halal importing authority that has accredited him and more broadly and fundamentally the requirement of the *Sharia* standard(s).

In western countries' markets halal certification may appear in various forms and be applied or rendered in different ways. The most common is the official standard form for meat exports which is issued at the end or towards the end halal production and processing and then accompanies as an endorsed certificate the halal products to their final destinations or sales outlet(s). Often if not always it is a document in multiple copies (a quadruplicate in Australia) signed by the competent government authority and the halal certifier and authenticated by the halal originating business enterprise (see appendix 1). A different but related certificate is called the Interim/Transfer certificate which is issued by an accredited halal certifier (See appendix 2). It is not strictly an official certificate and can not therefore be used as an export certificate or a final certificate for sale of a product as halal. However it is a key document that accompanies the movement and storage of the product at different locations in order to maintain its halal status and integrity and particularly to prevent it from mixing with non-halal or haram products. Underlying this process is the fundamental requirement that the premises in which the halal meat is produced or stored must be registered as a halal establishment in the form of a Certificate of Registration issued by an accredited halal certifier or competent halal authority. Operationally the principle of separation of halal from non-halal is of utmost importance and must be strictly observed. In storage, signage of the halal space or position must be bold and prominent where non-halal is present. Pork is a different matter altogether. According to most authorities, it must not be stored or displayed anywhere near a halal product and must not be produced held or processed in a halal registered establishment.

Another form of certification applied mainly to processed food rather than to meat *per se* relies on the official registration of the halal producing premises as a halal site and then issuing a halal certificate validating specific halal products produced in that site at any given time. In both meat and processed food, supervision and monitoring of process are required as essential conditions of product certification. Certification process in the case of meat requires intensive and rigorous application. Strict adherence to Islamic rites in slaughtering animals is the most prominent feature of this process. Certification in the case of processed food is somewhat different and may be more or less complex. Generally canned and packaged food requires investigation and approval of all the flavours ingredients and other additives, including meat, that go into the composition of the product. In some cases simply a declaration of the ingredients, if they are all halal, may be sufficient to obtain halal approval. This kind of food may require less frequency of supervision than fresh meat and instead may rely on more strict control and laboratory testing of ingredients at the approval stage and following that on standard monitoring and audit from time to time. There is considerable scope for an enterprise to strategically use halal on its product label in a way that serves both as a halal certificate and a symbol to attract halal customers.

Yet another form of certification which is not a strictly speaking an official or endorsed certificate is nonetheless used to serve a similar function but one which is purely declaratory in its objective. Aimed principally to attract the attention of the halal consumer, it is often issued by a self-appointed or unknown certifier or product manufacturer and sometimes by an officially approved and accredited entity. This form of certification appears as a halal logo on packaged/ bottled products with the word halal mostly in Arabic and sometimes both in Arabic and English as a prominent feature inscribed on the product label. Sometimes such logos and inscriptions are legitimate and have a traceable origin- even though it is not clear on the label. At other times their source, their ownership and who authorised it are difficult to trace with the label offering no guide as to its origin (see appendix 5). It is not uncommon to find the latter products on the shelves of major supermarkets in Australia. One can only surmise they are equally preponderant in the supermarkets of other major western countries. Validation that is used and rendered this way in the marketplace is highly likely to indicate fundamental flaws in the management and control over the halal certification process. It creates sufficient doubt for many Muslims to avoid these products or to consider them at least as non-halal. These unapproved halal certification practices can be damaging to the halal system and undermine consumer confidence in legitimate halal certification. They need to be brought under control by competent authorities.

There are both genuine and traceable logos and dubious non-traceable logos on the product labels on supermarket shelves in Australia alongside those that carry no halal logo. For the halal consumer his/her interest does not lie in those products that do not carry a halal logo or certificate but those that do from which he/she can make her choices. Take instant noodles and cheese for example. There are a wide range of noodle brands available in both major supermarkets: Coles and Woolworths. The only brand that carries a halal logo of any kind is imported from Indonesia: a two minute noodle of various flavours. The other brands whether Australian made or imported are not halal compliant products and therefore have no need for a halal logo, if they are not targeting halal consumers. However it is interesting that Nestlé's "Maggi Noodles" one of the biggest brands in instant noodles in Australia bears no halal logo at all, even though it is very familiar with halal and has utilised it in the past and probably still does for some of its other products from time to time.

By contrast the instant noodle brand *Indomie*- claimed to be the world's largest instant manufacturer- bears a halal logo. At once distinguished by the clarity of its design and the unambiguous source of its issuance, it leaves no doubt that it has been validated by a legitimate and well known authority with the expectation that it shall give the utmost confidence to halal consumers to purchase *Indomie* instant noodle products. This simple well designed halal logo has the word halal in English inscribed at the top of the logo and LPPM (the Indonesian acronym for the validating authority) and a numerical code at the bottom with three concentric circles in the middle. Inscribed in the middle of the two outer circles is the name of the approving authority "Majelis Ulama Indonesia" in English and the word halal in Arabic lodged in the centre of the circle (see Appendix 4). The Majelis (or council) is well known religious authority responsible for halal control and management in Indonesia.

If we compare this with the cheese brands available in both supermarkets we find that as with the instant noodles all except one do not have a halal logo- among 14 mainly Australian brands which I have cursorily examined. The exception in this case is the *Coon* brand's product line, cheddar cheese slices of Dairy Farmers Company; other *Coon* cheese types do not have a halal logo. The halal logo's anomaly in this case is striking. The outer package (of the 12, 24 and 36 slice packages) has no halal logo. Only the inside slice packages do. But the problem is that this is completely hidden by the labeling on the outside packaging (see appendix 5). Hence, a halal customer would in no way see the halal inscription inside. Why then one might ask would a firm go to the trouble of utilising a halal logo presumably at considerable expense when the very people to whom it is targeted are not going to see it at all? Equally if not more striking is that the halal logo, a simple light blue circle with the word halal in Arabic written inside it and in English underneath it, is not on the face of it traceable to its source. It bears no indication that it has been approved by a competent authority or accredited entity- unlike the *Indomie* noodle brand which does. In fact there is no claim that it has been approved by anyone! In the circumstances a logo of this kind can have no validity, appears to be deceptive and may do more harm than good for the halal industry. In the case of yogurt, none of the six brands on the supermarket shelves in Coles and Woolworth's, which I inspected in late 2011, had a halal logo. A year earlier I had observed that a Coles brand had one but it appears to have been removed. This haphazard application and rendering of halal is a striking illustration of how poorly companies are utilising it and how uncertain they are about managing it to their advantage.

A properly halal registered enterprise will be well advised to avoid the pitfalls of halal certification. Most importantly it can do so by ascertaining the credentials, the credibility and integrity of the halal certifier(s) it wishes to use. It is not always the case that the most amenable, the cheapest in price or the least rigorous of them is the most desirable or can provide optimal professional services. It should therefore be careful in choosing its preferred certifier. The possession by a prospective certifier of the following attributes or criteria may assist in making that choice:

- Approval or accreditation by major overseas halal authorities with the widest possible global market access
- Good knowledge of halal and haram in Islam including *Sharia*-based halal standards
- Good reputation with religious and professional integrity
- Good verbal and written communication skills including cross cultural communication skills
- Competence in auditing, monitoring and supervision of halal products
- Basic understanding of the needs of business in adopting halal standards and regulatory requirements
- Competence to provide advice and render practical assistance to business to comply fully with the halal standard
- Knowledge of and ability to provide a high standard of halal services
- Be able to provide training in halal rules and procedures
- Engagement in and ability to contribute to the development of international trade & commerce in halal goods and services
- Ability to provide access to halal markets

It would be wrong to say with any degree of confidence that the majority of current halal certifiers would be able to meet all or most of these criteria. There is a widely held view among Muslims that very few of them can do so. Nonetheless these are not unreasonable expectations for them to satisfy. Islam would require them to provide a high standard of service and possess an equally high level of competence. The reality is sharply different. In essence Islamic requisite criteria are being compromised by appointing in many cases less than competent certifiers. The best that an enterprise can do in this situation is to choose a certifier who is comparably better in meeting these criteria- certainly not an easy task! Exposing such deficiencies is necessary in the hope that those in authority may be prompted to act.

Categories of Halal Consumers: Multiple Identities

In Islam halal is a universal concept. It does not apply only to Muslim consumers but to the whole of mankind. In reality however halal consumers are at present overwhelmingly Muslim consumers. To say that is an important qualification. There are a small but steadily increasing numbers of non-Muslim halal consumers in western countries. A few are strictly halal consumers by choice. The overwhelming majority are product consumers by choice- products which happen to have a halal status. But product type alone is not a determinant of consumer choice; its characteristics and/or attributes are also to greater or lesser extent significant determinants of choice. Some non-Muslim halal consumers have no objection to buying halal designated products while others, the majority, are largely unaware of the halal character of the products they buy. Where they are aware they are generally indifferent to the halal status of the product but may choose it or come to like it for various reasons including its brand appeal, price, quality, trends, convenience, proximity etc. This varied category of non-Muslim halal consumers can be classified into the following sub-categories:

1. Those that are aware that the product is halal and consciously buy it
2. Those that are aware that the product is halal but are indifferent and buy it anyway
3. Those that buy a halal product without being aware that it is a halal product

A good example of the first sub-category can be found in the butcher shop where I buy halal meat in Melbourne on a weekly basis. It has two bold and prominent halal inscriptions on its front window and other smaller ones besides. This however does not deter many non-Muslim customers from purchasing their weekly meat in-take from this shop. There are three other butchers shops in close proximity- all within a walking distance- and two supermarkets close by. But it does a brisk trade and appears to have more culturally and ethnically diverse customers than all the other butchers in meat sales-comprising both Muslim and non-Muslim customers. What attracts the non-Muslim customers to this halal butcher more than to other non-halal butchers is not clear.

It is almost certainly not solely because it is halal- signifying both the method of slaughter and the absence of pork- which is the very reason which attracts Muslim halal consumers. There may be an element of indifference which accounts for their attraction, as exhibited prominently by the second category above. There may also be other influences such as perceived quality, novelty, service or atmosphere etc. present in the choice. Price however is not one of these influences as it is almost the same in all other competing shops. There may well be a closer affinity in identity between this sub-category and the second, and on closer examination they may be found to have similar characteristics and to exhibit similar behaviour at least in some important respects. There is need for further research to throw light on this and other related issues. The purpose of this paper is simply to identify them, and to recognise them together with other sub-categories, as an important component of halal customers.

The second sub-category shares some characteristics with the first and others with third. Both the second and first are conscious that the product they are buying is halal although they buy it for different reasons- the one because he/she wants to buy a halal product and the other by way of indifference whether it is halal or not. The second category is influenced by various characteristics of the product, not it would appear by its halal attribute- a characteristic he shares with the third. He/ She considers the halal attribute as being irrelevant to his/her choice. But importantly his/her attitude and responses to it are not negative, and in view of the fact that he/she buys it, can only be considered to be positive. The second category may also have close characteristics with non-Muslim halal consumers who work or reside in Muslim and Muslim majority countries- a sub-category not included in the above classification. It can be reasonably argued that these consumers are generally unconcerned about the halal attribute, and may in fact be favourably disposed to it, since most or all of the food products sold in these countries are considered halal.

Unlike the first and the second categories, the third is unaware of the halal attribute and it is unknown what his response would be if he was. It is very likely it would not be of concern, because his responses to products and their appeal to him would have been honed in practice by repeat purchases over time- perhaps over many years. Observation of consumer purchases of halal labeled products on supermarket shelves indicates this to be the case. His attachment to a brand or a product label he is accustomed to buy is unlikely to be changed in normal circumstances by finding out that it has a halal inscription or attribution. Overall, his lack of awareness insulates him from being influenced by the halal attribute either way- to buy it or not to buy it. He is therefore willing to buy the product irrespective whether it is inscribed halal or has a halal status or not. Nevertheless, his consumption of halal products -albeit unconsciously- qualifies him to be included as one of the subcategories of halal consumers identified above.

By simple observation, it appears that the third category is numerically the largest and it is where further growth is likely to be most dramatic in the short to medium term. There are strong indications of this in the marketplace. In Australia as in other western countries like the U.S and Britain there are many products on supermarket shelves with halal status and/ or display a halal logo or inscription. These are often familiar products to non-Muslim customers, which products they have regularly bought over the years. They buy these products irrespective of whether they are halal or not. Halal therefore is not a barrier to the choice consumers make in purchasing these products. The indifference exhibited towards a particular characteristic or attribute of the product- albeit an important one- is not at all surprising. In the case of halal, very few would know its significance or meaning. Looked at from this perspective it can reasonably be assumed that its impact on the exercise of consumer choice for this sub-category of halal consumers can be said at least in one respect to be neutral. In other words its presence in the form of inscription in no way detracts from the factors that underlie the appeal of that product for the consumer.

In another respect the validation of halal products in this way has a dramatic impact in the rendering and sale of products in the global marketplace. It removes a formidable barrier to market access simply by adopting a strategic application of the ethic and instrument of halal certification – a barrier which would not have been possible to remove otherwise. Once this is achieved, product attributes can be said to be more or less equalised from a Muslim perspective, so that they are made to compete on what in popular parlance is termed "a level playing field". In other words the absence of halal status or identity no longer prevents a category or categories of halal consumers from purchasing it. There are also many other examples of products without halal inscription on supermarket shelves that are purchased by non-Muslim customers to which halal certification can be applied at the manufacturing stage. This points to, the possibility that there may be considerable scope for firms to extend their production of goods and services to a broader and growing "halal" customer base than has been the case in the past.

These are not permanent sub-categories in halal consumer divisions, conceptually or in practice. Instead they are malleable and shifting categories that will be influenced by a range of factors overtime. The most prominent and long lasting in its impact is the increasing knowledge and awareness of halal certified products and services. This will have the greatest impact on the third sub-category. The peculiarity of its current predominance in numerical strength based as it is on lack of awareness of halal status or attribute of products is however unlikely to be tenable in the long term. As more consumers become aware of halal products, its numerical strength will gradually wane. And while it may not completely disappear in the short to medium term, there is likely to be a gradual shift away from it to the second and first categories- with probably the second becoming the most dominant in the long term. How levels of awareness of halal and perceptions about it will impact among these categories of consumers, however, remains to be seen.

These sub-categories of halal consumers have neither been given any exposure, nor have they been recognised at all. As halal consumers they are in fact unidentified and it appears largely undiscovered in any literature as a category or subcategory. The vast number of traditional halal consumers has thrown a long shadow over them and obscured their existence and enterprises on the whole may have been complicit if for no other reason than that they could not or would not integrate them into their conception of halal consumers or planning processes. Their important role in the marketplace must be brought into view and their influence and purchasing power recognised. There is need to explore how they make their decisions and what motivates or drives their behaviour or otherwise. Their difference from the norm must also be given proper acknowledgement. If we accept these propositions, they will no doubt bring about dramatic changes to the way we think about halal and halal consumers. Fundamental to this thinking of the new category is to consider in the first instance changes to the traditional definition and conception of who a halal consumer is and in the second instance formulate a better alternative to more accurately reflect the composition, scope and dynamic of modern halal consumers. In this context the new halal consumers are no longer simply Muslim consumers, rather they are global consumers comprising both Muslim and non-Muslim consumers.

Halal Consumers: A Changing Definition?

In light of these developments, the identity and the popular conception of who halal consumers are needs to be modified, even redefined. Though the halal concept and its foundations remain unchanged, its uses and apprehension by both consumers and producers have arguably radically shifted or about to do so. Halal consumers are no longer solely Muslim consumers as has been understood to be the case in the past, but include a significant and growing minority of non-Muslim consumers from all parts of the globe. Halal compliant products and services are not therefore exclusively targeted to Muslim markets and to Muslim consumers in them but increasingly to all markets and to all consumers that are willing to buy them. This indicates a movement away from the present narrow conception to a broader more universal conception of halal consumers, which is closer to and more aligned with the original Islamic conception of halal consumers as universal consumers. In order to acknowledge the shift in the composition, scope and identity of halal consumers and to set the parameters of discussion and analysis for further research, we put forward the following tentative definition: A halal consumer may be defined as a person or entity that purchases or otherwise utilises goods and/or services which have a halal status or comply with a halal standard and may be certified according to and in compliance with the *Sharia* (Muslim Law). What is significant about this definition is the absence of the term Muslim in reference to consumers and its replacement with halal. The importance of the change is not to minimise the importance of Muslim consumers, whose role remains dominant, but underscore the fact that there are other halal consumers who in fact buy halal and whose wants need to be taken into account by firms in producing goods and services. The definitional change also underscores the fact that the original apprehension does not fully conform with current reality and that its particularist and exclusivist connotations are no longer valid to reflect actual consumer behaviour in the marketplace.

The pattern of consumption of halal goods and services by the two major categories of halal consumers- Muslim and non-Muslim- is not always the same but is often dictated by very different influences, in which cultural norms and current styles or trends and attendant meanings are dominant. The same may be true among the sub-categories of halal consumers. This does not detract from the fact that halal is based on Islamic ethical system and values. It is therefore reasonable to say that halal may not have the same signification nor carry the same meanings or attract the same level of commitment from the various categories of halal consumers. The values they espouse may be different to a greater or lesser degree. However, they are bonded by the fact that they all buy the same halal products consciously or unconsciously and enterprises respond to them as being halal consumers without actually distinguishing who they are and to which category or subcategory they belong. Islamic values have always had a universal focus. Such integrated and composite apprehension and rendering of halal consumers is not inconsistent with Islamic outlook which espouses universal values. Islam first and foremost addresses itself to mankind and the principles of both halal and halal consumers have a universal reference.

Consequences of the New Definition of Halal Consumers

There are important consequences that follow from these new sub-categories of halal consumers for the production and sale of goods and services by firms interested in halal markets in their broadest global sense. In the context of decision making, they represent demand for goods and services that had not hitherto been apparent, and if apparent not sufficiently recognised or appreciated. At best they have been subsumed perhaps unjustifiably, under the traditional category of halal consumers. The strong and continuing growth in both the traditional and the relatively new halal consumers worldwide means that firms must respond accordingly and consider significantly expanding their production of some goods and services than they had hitherto by utilising halal certification as strategic tool. This would enable them to grasp the new realities and reflect the identity, composition as well the purchasing habits of modern halal consumers and to embrace a much more dynamic apprehension of how they are constituted and dispersed globally in market settings. It is no longer sufficient nor true to say that a halal consumers are solely Muslim consumers or restricted to a particular religiously observant Muslim consumers. The fact is that many non-Muslim halal consumers are purchasing significant quantities of halal products without them being recognised or acknowledged. There is a strong and continuing growth in halal consumption by Muslim consumers but the most prominent is that which is brought about by halal certification on the one hand and the emergence of the new categories of halal consumers on the other.

Many companies are unaware of these trends and are not therefore taking advantage of the wide expansion of and strong growth in halal consumption among Muslims and non-Muslims. It appears however that there are others who have recognised the change in realities and are doing so. As a result they are responding in novel and different ways and developing strategies to capture an ever larger share of the broader conception of halal consumers. At the forefront of the latter are halal abattoirs in Australia. Packaged food processors are not far behind and are increasingly responding to changes in the expanded horizon of halal consumers- albeit tentatively and cautiously. However it is not absolutely clear whether the responses by enterprises are due to either the growing demand pressures from traditional halal consumers or from the new halal consumers or both. It is possible that the extent of awareness and the strength of demand from the latter are somewhat overstated. It may also be characterised merely as passive or soft rather than active demand. This characterisation is posited merely to distinguish firms responding to demand pressures emanating from traditional halal consumers and the strategic imperatives of firms in wanting to maximise their sales outcomes by taking advantage of and becoming active participants in the creation, growth and expansion of the new halal consumers. Be that it may, there has been and continues to be evidence of growing demand from and/or increasing sales to both categories of halal consumers.

About forty years ago halal red meat exports by Australian abattoirs was an insignificant component of overall red meat exports. The overwhelming majority of abattoirs did not produce it for local consumption either, as the population of traditional Muslim consumers was very small. There was little knowledge about halal markets and demand for halal meat was conceptually difficult to grasp and in practice even more difficult to meet. As demand strengthened and abattoirs became familiar with halal they also became increasingly aware that the two markets are not necessarily mutually exclusive if approached from the halal perspective and that the same product can be offered to consumers in both the halal and non-halal markets. Such an approach would have minimal or no negative impact on the operations of the abattoir but the most maximum positive impact in expanding its global access to markets and the scope of its customers in Australia. This striking outcome is made possible by abattoirs' adoption of halal as the preferred method of their operations. Both in Australia and overseas their customer base was limited in the past to one category of customers, with the adoption of the halal approach that limitation is completely removed and the abattoir now has the potential to capture the maximum number of customers globally and locally-be they Muslim or non-Muslim.

As a result of the increased understanding of halal, many red meat export abattoirs in Australia produce meat for diverse export markets and for a similarly diverse local market. What is striking about them is the broad scope of their current customers, compared to the past, and their geographical spread, dispersed across more than one hundred countries – with Muslim countries showing more robust demand than non-Muslim countries (Meat and Livestock Australia 2012). Barring seasonal and climatic changes the strength of this trend is continuing and is reflected in the strong growth of red meat exports, particularly lamb and mutton to Middle East and other predominantly Muslim markets. For example, in the financial year 2007 to 2008, Australian lamb exports to the Middle East increased 18 per cent from 20,122 Mt to 23,747 Mt and beef sales increased 130 per cent from 3,356 MT TO 7,718 Mt. The region maintained its position as Australia's biggest mutton market, up 3 per cent from 50,000 Mt to 52,188 Mt. Most prominently in 2007 the UAE emerged as Australia's second largest lamb export market after the United States (Meat and Livestock Australia 2010). The results were even better in 2009 as the table below shows (United States department of Agriculture 2010). Emphasising the importance of the region for Australia, Meat and Livestock Australia states that, "The Middle East market is Australia's largest live sheep and sheep meat destination. The greatest increase in volumes sold for all species was in the UAE" (Meat and Livestock Australia 2010). More than any other instrument, this dramatic increase in demand for Australian halal meat exports to Muslim and Muslim majority countries is due solely to halal certification, without which there would have been no meat exports to these countries.

Table 2 Australian Lamb & Mutton Exports for Dec. 2009

(Metric Tons)	Dec 2009	YTD 2009	YTD 2008	YTD Change
Lamb Exports				
U.S.	3,008	38,328	36,855	4.0%
Middle East	2,943	35,870	25,368	41.4%
E.U.	1,052	13,722	11,602	18.3%
China	888	13,863	14,041	-1.3%
All Others	5,360	63,252	63,742	-0.8%
Total Lamb	13,251	165,035	151,608	8.9%
Mutton Exports				
Middle East	5,173	51,895	50,490	2.8%
U.S.	1,755	10,800	13,415	-19.5%
South Africa	78	4,439	13,680	-67.6%
Taiwan	795	7,739	7,501	3.2%
All Others	5,821	59,106	72,603	-18.6%
Total Mutton	13,622	133,979	157,689	-15.0%

Source: *Department of Agriculture, Fisheries, and Forestry*

In most major halal importing markets the overwhelming majority of halal meat customers are obviously Muslim; however a small minority comprises the new category of non-Muslim halal customers identified above- customers that buy halal products for various reasons other than for religious values, affiliation or commitment. The reverse is true in Australia and other major western countries except for the fact that non-Muslim halal consumers account for a significant growth in halal consumption. If this trend in the growth of halal consumers continues, it is not inconceivable that, in the long term, Muslims will become a minority of halal consumers of certain products such as lamb in many western countries like Australia and non-Muslims the majority. The reasons why this seeming anomaly whereby the majority of halal customers are non-Muslim Australians may arise are threefold. Firstly the emergence of and the strong growth in the three sub-categories of halal consumers described above; secondly the trend by major halal registered enterprises to produce and the major supermarkets chains and other sales outlets to source most of their products including meat, and many other packaged products from the halal compliant establishments; and thirdly the influence of halal certification as a strategic tool to capture as many customers as possible globally. Continuation of this trend would also show the huge impact of these previously unidentified sub-categories of non-Muslim halal consumers on trade and commerce in halal goods and services, and on how halal is apprehended and rendered in the marketplace.

What gives these abattoirs this unprecedented versatility is the strategic choice they have made to adopt the halal standard for all their meat production. Consistent with this approach they have decided to register as halal establishments, employ halal slaughtermen and supervisors and produce their meat under a halal program supervised by both the Australian Quarantine and Inspection Service (AQIS) and an approved halal certifier. They have adopted the halal system as a whole for rational economic reasons in that it is at least as profitable if not a great deal more profitable than the alternative. The production of goods under this system has the potential to result in huge increases in the number of their customers. Both in export and local consumption they produce for undifferentiated halal customers both Muslim and non-Muslim. In orientation they respond to changes that are taking place in a globally integrated market. Halal registered abattoirs and the two major supermarkets in Australia- Coles and Woolworths- are good examples of this trend. Coles sources almost all the lamb meat it sells from just two of these abattoirs- one of which is CRF Colac P/L. The same is true of Woolworths whose lamb supply comes from a similarly narrow field of halal registered establishments. The abattoir in each case produces and processes meat as halal, but the supermarket sells it as non-halal. The supermarket could however sell the products as halal if it so wished- subject to meeting certain minimum halal requirements unrelated to the status of meat itself but to its handling. This offers the supermarket the flexibility and the choice to sell its lamb products as halal or non-halal. It is however this kind of abattoir and many others like it that is setting a new trend and creating a new robust and versatile model for the future operations of halal establishments and the sale of halal goods and services. The same strategy is being applied to the export of Lamb and mutton. There is no reason why it could not be applied to many other products that require halal compliance with similar effect. The versatility of the new type of abattoir is at once impressive in its integrative capacity and far reaching in its outcomes compared to its non-halal counterparts. For example it can produce lamb or mutton:

- To meet direct export orders from overseas halal and non-halal markets
- To meet orders from Australian exporters to overseas halal and non-halal markets
- To supply to supermarket chains in Australia and overseas who may choose to sell the product as halal or non-halal
- To supply local outlets such as butchers and boning rooms who may sell the product as halal or non-halal

Conclusion

The whole complex of innovation and strategy underpinning this approach to globalising halal is brought about by the application of halal certification. Its impact is therefore highly significant and consequential. Without it there would be little or no access of goods and services claiming to have halal status to halal markets. On the one hand there is the likelihood that governments may prevent their entry into halal markets and on the other even if entry is granted that halal consumers may not buy them or have confidence in buying them. The sensitivity of this issue is exemplified most vividly in both the Indonesian and UAE cases cited in this paper. The value and efficacy of halal certification is to eliminate or reduce problems of market access and to dispel any doubts that customers may have about halal status of goods and services. Most importantly halal certification serves to cement the relationship between enterprises that produce halal goods and services and halal customers. No other instrument has the capacity to engender confidence and thereby satisfy the wants of halal customers and increase sales outcomes as halal certification does. Without it, firms would have a narrower customer base and much less ability or opportunity for expansion. By contrast certification offers the greatest scope for development. It provides access to markets that producers would not otherwise have and consequently the potential of massive expansion of customers. It is a striking illustration of how companies can respond intelligently and creatively to modern markets.

For these and other reasons halal certification is an extremely valuable strategy to maximize commercial opportunities, and an indispensable tool to expand, entrench and satisfy halal consumer demand globally. A crucial element in this reorientation and thinking about halal consumers is to recognise the shift that has occurred in the definition of who they are and embracing the fundamental changes in their identity that is only now becoming apparent. It is also important to apprehend how they are dispersed across market settings. In this new rendering, halal consumers are no longer only Muslim consumers but global consumers willing to buy halal products and services. Also important is to recognise the strong growth in the consumption of halal goods and services brought about by the strong growth in traditional halal consumers and the emergence of the new halal consumers. Together, these complementary categories revolutionise our thinking and understanding of halal consumers and halal markets. They enable firms to respond to global markets more effectively and more efficiently than they had done in the past.

Chapter 3

Meat and Livestock Australia's Global Halal Brand: A brand to be ... or not to be

Introduction: MLA Halal Brand Project

On the 9th of October 2008 Meat and livestock Australia (MLA) announced that its "unique [Halal] brand that was developed last year ... for use in the Middle East red meat market has now gone global". MLA is a producer owned organisation for red meat and livestock industry. According to its website, it provides marketing and research services to the entire red meat industry in Australia, including livestock producers. It works closely with the Federal Government in most areas of its activities, particularly in halal meat exports. Together with thirteen or so "Islamic societies" that comprise all halal certifiers in Australia, it is also a member Halal Consultative Committee under the chairmanship and guidance of the Federal Government represented by the Australian Quarantine and Inspection Service (AQIS). AQIS is the government authority that regulates and overseas all food exports from Australia.

This paper examines various aspects of MLA's global halal brand: first and foremost how the brand came to be and what its claims are. Since the key claim is that it is a halal brand, it examines in particular, if the claim is legitimate. In that context it explores key questions of how the brand is constituted, and given identity, legitimacy and credibility. It finds that there are serious problems with the very conception, use and rendering of the MLA brand. It argues that these problems stem in part from the fact that there is no model, or paradigm on which the MLA brand is based though this in itself is no barrier to its construction or realisation as a halal brand. It also stems in part from MLA failure to make sufficient enquiry to formulate its brand project and plan its implementation. It is clear that MLA has relied on halal product certification approach to validate and construct its brand project. The paper shows how wrong this approach is. Importantly, the paper also shows how MLA could have avoided the problems inherent in its approach and offers an alternative course of action upon which to construct a soundly based, legitimate halal brand.

The Power of Brand and its Compatibility with Halal

Branding can be a powerful tool for the sale and marketing of goods and services. The MLA halal brand is no ordinary brand; it is ambitious in scope and unique in its identity as well as in how that identity is constituted. If it is designed, developed and marketed properly a halal brand can be a very powerful brand in that it can potentially offer a corporation's products immediate access to a huge market of approximately 1.7 billion Muslim consumers worldwide. However, brand and halal are not, in all cases and in all circumstances, a natural fit nor are they always compatible. There are in fact circumstances in which they can be and others they are not compatible. Halal can not be made to cohere conceptually or in practice with brand by fiat. The condition of compatibility can only be attained in Australia and other non-Muslim countries to the extent that products or services bearing the halal brand satisfy halal compliance requirements embedded in the *Sharia* (Muslim Law) and validated by a competent halal authority. Even then it is not free from being contested and its credibility questioned.

Maintaining Halal Integrity

For business enterprises it is very important to understand first and foremost that the concept of halal is not amenable to preconceived notions of marketing. In fact the reverse; marketing or any commercial activity must abide by the rules and expectation of halal to qualify for halal status. To use it purely as a strategic marketing tool is not only to misunderstand halal but also to misrepresent it. The danger in strategic constructions of this kind is that it has the potential to devalue the concept of halal and to discredit the application and the uses that are made of it. Those enterprises that want to utilise halal properly should exercise caution in the way they think about it and even more so the way they apply it as a validating instrument of the halal status of their products and services. Manipulation of the concept in ways that are inconsistent with its religious underpinnings and endowing it instead with purely marketing strategic imperatives is a very risky exercise that is highly questionable in the *Sharia* and is likely to be contested vigorously on this basis.

Combining Halal and Brand: a Cautionary Note

What is striking about MLA's adoption and utilisation of a halal brand is that it is the first time that halal and brand have been combined in Australia to form a composite concept and the first time it has been used as a validating instrument. The only other entity, I am aware of, that has utilised and applied the concept of a global halal brand is the Sultanate of Brunei. We will not consider the Brunei brand in this section as it is dealt with elsewhere in this book. Here we need only point out that Brunei has been working on the project for a considerably longer time before it was made operational and its outcome to-date, as a halal brand, remains uncertain. It is also important to point out that although they share a common bond as brands and claims to halal status, they are different in many respects and represent different brand models. The Brunei brand has a different identity and a much broader scope and objectives than the MLA brand. Its foundation as a halal brand however appears sound.

The relationship of halal and brand has never before been explored nor used as composite term conceptually or in practice in Australia. What is interesting therefore is the boldness and confidence with which MLA has applied the composite term as a purely marketing tool. Is that confidence well placed or misplaced? Are there issues that need to be explored before utilising the halal brand? Is there compelling research or knowledge that informs the validation of the brand project or an authoritative endorsement upon which it relies? Or is it just that it seemed to be such a good marketing idea at the time and nothing else? Because of the total absence of information from the MLA, a certain level of speculation can not be avoided.

Figure 3 MLA's halal brand from its website (2012)

Reflections on how the Halal Brand Came to Be

It is inconceivable that MLA adopted the halal meat brand without endorsement by a Muslim entity or entities with the appropriate authority to do so. It would be folly to have done so. This however can not be discounted in part because of the obscure way the MLA halal brand has come about and in part because of the absence of any reference to an authorising or accrediting entity. Barring that, there are only two possible sources from which endorsement could have been obtained for a project of this kind: halal certifier(s) in Australia or overseas halal authorities. There is no reason to presume and certainly no indication in MLA publicly released documents that overseas halal authorities' approval was either sought or obtained individually or collectively. In light of this, the most likely scenario is that MLA had instead sought and obtained this endorsement from the majority or all of the thirteen, or so, societies that comprise the halal certifying bodies in Australia. If the majority of the societies approved it, it would be the first time a collective decision of this nature and this scope has ever been made by the certifiers in Australia, or by halal certifiers elsewhere in the world. In fact, there is no effective unifying instrument or entity with an Islamic reference through which such an approval can be granted. And if it is the case it had been granted as a concession to MLA it would be wrong to do so as a matter of principle because it would imply a special privilege granted to it and not to others which is contrary to halal as a universal system. Given these considerations, it is reasonable to presume that endorsement was granted, if at all, after pressures were brought to bear upon these societies. Whether that is the case or not, the question which immediately arises is: do these societies individually or collectively have the authority to validate, approve or certify the "MLA halal brand".

Validity of the Construction of MLA Halal Brand

If the societies had endorsed the brand at all it could have occurred in the context of the only forum which brings together the government, the Islamic societies and the MLA- i.e. the Halal Consultative Committee, under the auspices of AQIS- which AQIS itself has created and which it regularly convenes and chairs its meetings. On the face of it, this forum is certainly not the appropriate forum to make this determination as it is purely a consultative forum. Furthermore, the legal control and influence over which the government body exercises over halal certifiers through this instrument are obvious and so too is the close relationship it has with the potential direct beneficiary of this determination-the MLA. The presumed presence and participation of both MLA and the government in decision making in this forum, therefore gives rise to serious issues of conflict of interest which would potentially nullify any decision regarding this matter in this forum or in any other fora where they are present. It points to broader problems inherent in the formulation, construction and rationalisation of the said forum and the certifier's membership in it. It is important to establish the locus of this decision-making, because it does not appear that endorsement of the brand by this means is soundly based as it is doubtful that it is within the competence of the societies individually or collectively. And if it is the case that this determination was made in the said forum it simply wrong to do so, on the grounds of propriety alone.

Underlying Weaknesses in Construction

One of the most distinguishing characteristics of MLA is that it does not itself produce, manufacture and/or export halal meat, whereas many of its members do. This obvious difference explains a great deal why granting halal approval of members is not, with proper guidance, difficult to obtain whereas halal approval of the MLA brand is problematic, not least because there is no single identifiable entity or precedent to rely on to have the brand approved as halal or halal compliant. The stark difference between halal approved companies and the MLA is that the former have products to be certified halal and premises to be registered as halal establishments where production takes place; the latter has neither. This distinction is highly significant. The mistakes made by the MLA are largely a consequence of its failure to fully grasp or take sufficient account of this distinction. This does not mean as a matter of principle that there are no bases for an MLA brand to gain halal status and become halal compliant, only that it has not done so in the appropriate manner. Beyond that it depends on whether the relevant competent halal authority, on considering MLA application, is satisfied that it meets prescribed halal standard(s). In the first instance consideration by a competent authority in this regard is not so much about certifying a halal product or registering a halal establishment, but about approving a halal symbol and the uses that will be made of that symbol in applying it to halal products and services.

A company that produces halal meat obtains two types of approval. Firstly the premises where halal is produced are registered-separately if they are at different locations- as halal establishments and secondly, the slaughter of the animals, the preparation of the meat and the processes associated with its production are approved as halal by halal certifiers that are characterised as but are not in most cases Islamic Societies. This is done after a comprehensive program had been approved as part of a first step by a company to register and apply for halal status for its products. There are further processes downstream. Even in terms of normal processes of halal certification MLA approach is highly irregular and certainly not in accord with common halal norms and practices. MLA does not itself produce or own the products for which it is seeking halal certification. Rather what it is seeking is *post facto* halal approval for a brand complex wholly of its own conception and making, which is quite a different proposition altogether.

The role of Islamic societies can sometimes cause confusion. Despite their role as certifiers, these societies are distinct from halal authorities. Overseas halal authorities in major halal importing countries approve individual Islamic societies in Australia and elsewhere and accredit them to certify their halal meat imports. Yet the distinction is lost completely when some Islamic societies act as if they are or wrongly claim to be halal authorities by for example expressing this in their name. The claim can lead to considerable confusion and/or misunderstanding among those who need to know- enterprises that produce and consumers that consume halal products and services- who these entities are and what are their roles and functions. It is the responsibility of both AQIS and major overseas halal authorities to offer a simple appropriate definition which distinguishes these entities and clarifies their relative functions. It may even be necessary in some circumstances to impose penalties on any Islamic society or a certifying body wrongfully claiming to be a halal authority. This is extremely important in order to prevent halal certifiers from exercising powers they do not have and ought not to have such as the approval of a halal brand, particularly a global one, without transparent and valid justification.

Weaknesses in Certification Structures

There are no uniform standards or criteria which overseas national halal authorities rely on to accredit halal certifiers. Looking at the types of organisations that have been accredited over the years, no pattern emerges which gives an indication of how it is done or what criteria are applied. There is distinct lack of transparency to hazard an opinion and a high probability there is little or no common ground on accreditation. Some overseas authorities accredit a relatively small number (four or five in the case of Saudi Arabia), others the majority (eleven to twelve) of the current halal certifiers (May 2008-May 2009). Among the most prominent feature of these societies are their low educational profile and their poor service provision to business enterprises. There is a widespread belief in the Muslim community that arbitrary accreditation has led over the years to poor performance and lack of accountability. It has also led to abuse of the system of certification in many ways. On crucial issues regarding certification for example some societies have made seriously flawed decisions which are contrary to accepted halal norms. In one case, documented in the report in this book, an Islamic Society granted halal registration to an establishment which produced pork (a haram product) in the same premises as it did halal. In another case the same society is reported to have granted halal certification/registration to a business (a food chain outlet) which itself claims that it does not produce or offer halal products for sale, has not applied for halal certification and does not even want to do so at present (*Hume Leader* 7 February 2012. See article in appendix 3.).What is clear is that such anomalies and abuses engender weaknesses in the system- which can be avoided. At the heart of these problems is the lack of proper transparent and knowledge-based criteria. And even though there is no specific accreditation granted by the majority of Muslim countries, that which is granted by the few major halal importing countries (namely, Saudi Arabia, UAE, Indonesia and Malaysia) is generally used as an instrument to cover most if not all countries to which halal goods are exported.

Be that it may, the important point is that the authority given to Islamic societies to certify is strictly limited to individual products such as meat on the basis of regulatory requirements of each halal importing country that had accredited them for this purpose. To act outside the parameters of product based certification is to exercise powers they do not have now and have never had in the past. Overseas halal authorities not only confer local certifiers with the authority to certify, they can also withdraw or cancel that authority without reference to or consultation with any other entity. They merely inform halal exporting countries- AQIS in the case of Australia- that registration of a particular certifier has been withdrawn and can no longer certify products as halal on its behalf in regard to products or services imported into that country (See appendix 6 for AQIS list halal certifiers in Australia for 2010).

Table 3 The countries that accredit certifiers in Australia and numbers they accredit in each State

	NSW	Queensland	South Australia	Victoria	Western Australia	Total
Saudi Arabia	2	0	1	1	1	5
UAE	2	0	1	2	2	7
Indonesia	2*	1	1	2	4	10
Malaysia	2	1	1	2	5	11
Singapore	3	1	1	2	5	12

The number of certifiers varies from time to time. In early 2010 Indonesia added a new certifier to the accredited list.

Source: AQIS Meat Notice No: 2008 / 04; valid May 2008- May 2009

Limits of Certifiers' Role in Brand Construction

If it is the case that MLA relied on halal certifiers in Australia to endorse its halal brand concept it is hard to imagine how this could have come about. It is one thing for an approved Islamic society to certify halal products for export purposes, it is quite another for it to endorse a brand-its formation development and use as a halal brand. To do so would be to confuse product certification with the approval of a halal brand and its practical uses and applications. It should be clear that in endorsing the brand the societies would have in effect assumed a role they had not hitherto performed and for which presumably they have no authority. One probable explanation is that MLA has not sufficiently explored the basic issues that a halal brand would raise: for example what its claims are to being a halal brand as well as the criteria on which they are based and their credibility. Achieving credibility presupposes among other things that the brand has satisfied prescribed norms and standards based on the *Sharia* that would enable it to claim halal status. It also brings to the fore questions such as how the brand is evaluated to uphold its halal claims in the first instance and validate its halal practices on a continual basis in the second instance. If these are the fundamental questions which need to be addressed then it is obvious that the notion of a MLA halal brand and the uses made of it as a marketing tool are contestable to say the least.

The Process of Certification of Products for Export

Halal certification of exports is based on separate approval of each product or category of products by a competent certifier after it had undergone a monitoring and supervision process and had satisfied halal program requirements. The whole process culminates in the issuance of a government halal certificate for export purposes which carries three separate stamps: an MS (Muslim slaughtered) stamp referred to in the document as "Official Mark"; a federal government stamp referred to in the document as "Government Seal" and the competent certifying Islamic entity stamp referred to in the document as "Name of Islamic Organisation". This certificate in effect validates halal meat exports from Australia and halal meat sales in importing countries. It accompanies the halal product to its export destination without which the product would not be accepted as halal by the importing country. The new MLA devised brand is a different instrument from this kind of halal certification. At one level it sets aside and completely dispenses with the underlying processes necessary for halal certification, except those which its halal registered members are required to comply with. Paradoxically, at another level, it presents itself as an instrument that gathers all certification and approval process, and expresses them in a composite symbol encapsulated in and represented by the MLA halal brand. In other words it is far more comprehensive in its reach and scope than simply the conventional halal certificate (See appendix 1 for a halal certificate for meat).

Distinguishing Halal Brand from Halal Certification

The MLA halal brand differs radically from halal certification. It also constitutes a dramatic departure from the conventional way of gaining halal status. There is unmistakable conceptual and functional difference between the two. Basically one pertains to a physical phenomenon, a product to be traded; the other to its symbolic representation, utilised to maximise sales outcomes. Although MLA represents the red meat industry, it is a different entity from halal establishments that produce or export halal meat. Its halal brand is not based on products that it produces but on products that others do. The brand has no products of its own on the basis of which it can apply for halal certification or premises which produce halal and for which it can apply for halal registration. The brand therefore is removed spatially and conceptually from individually certified products belonging to specific companies. Despite this it relies solely on its role as a red meat industry organisation with voluntary membership to construct its brand project. Many of the enterprises it represents do not produce, nor would claim to produce halal products at all. Their relationship with those that produce halal is that they belong to the same industry group- the red meat industry. This commonality however does not constitute nor does it warrant a claim to a genuine shared identity from a halal perspective.

The brand which the MLA has constructed is not about certification at all, but about strategic marketing of products that had obtained halal certification. There is no other apparent justification for the MLA brand. This is a proposition with which the MLA may not disagree. However, presenting the issues in this way clarifies the project's aim; it also draws clear distinctions between the terms and their practical applications. The effect of this distinction is to shift the argument of the MLA halal brand from one about certification to one about branding and the moral and intellectual integrity of such branding. In this case branding has to be considered as a separate issue and the validity of the halal brand assessed on its own merits. The questions it raises are varied. They include the following:

1. Can a purely marketing brand be halal approved and are there conditions over and above the normal conditions it would be required to comply with?
2. Who endorsed the brand and validated it as a halal brand, on whose authority and on what criteria?
3. Did the MLA submit an application for halal approval and to which authority was that application submitted?
4. If the brand is approved halal by a competent authority how does MLA comply with halal standards and regulatory requirements?
5. Did MLA's application for halal approval of its brand include a halal program which outlines how the brand will be controlled, utilised and rendered in the marketplace?
6. If the approval of the halal brand was granted by a competent authority is it open-ended or subject to renewal?
7. Are its halal-brand activities monitored, audited or otherwise subjected to scrutiny and how?
8. What kind of media will be utilised and in what ways?

Unbundling Halal and Brand

It appears that the halal status of the MLA brand is not inherent in itself nor derived from legitimate authority; rather it is solely derived from the fact that some of the companies which MLA represents or is associated with produce certified halal products. What this demonstrates clearly is that there is no halal status conferred on or expressed in the brand itself other than the halal status granted to numerous establishments and products through legitimate certification. Now, it is not possible to have it both ways: to argue on the one hand that the brand is a separate issue from certifying products as halal and, on the other hand to assert that the halal status of the brand derives from the certification of these products. The logic of this striking duality is achieved by transferring individual product certification to endorse MLA brand project. The link established by this means is contrived and tenuous in the extreme. This form of bundling used commonly in as a marketing strategy to create "a complete product" is unsuitable for creating a halal brand.

Products categories that have been traditionally certified halal individually are now in the context of the MLA formulation combined, albeit in a brand complex, and impressed with a collective halal approval as an aggregate unit: no matter what species they are- cattle, sheep, goat, venison etc. This is in marked contrast to how halal approval had been done in the past and how it is done in the present. And it is interesting to note that the drivers of this dramatic change are not competent Muslim institutions but rather a non-Muslim entity that does not itself produce, control, process or directly own any halal products. It is remarkable that MLA sees fit to aggregate all of Australia's red meat exports to a particular region or globally into one indivisible basket of goods, validating them as having halal status by way of a halal brand that it had created. To capture such a vast array of products, species, production companies in a net of halal brand is manifestly problematic for any system let alone a halal system, without proper, indeed stringent controls.

Misrepresentation of Halal

Irrespective of how cleverly one may manipulate the concept of halal solely for commercial purposes, it should be obvious that brand has a different function, is a different phenomenon, and serves different purposes from halal certification except of course for the fact that you can apply halal to brand, subject to complying with relevant standards. None of the functions of the MLA halal brand, as far we are aware, include oversight or actual approval of halal products or practices. The halal certification system as it currently exists is applied only to processes of production and manufacturing of specific products, produced by a specific company at a given time and place, for human consumption. It is not possible to aggregate certification across establishments, across companies, across species without defined limits of time and most importantly without Muslim supervision and control of process to ensure compliance with halal standard(s).

A composite representation of this process on this scale by way of a brand, far removed from the production and manufacturing processes, is certainly contrary to traditional practice of halal certification as it is to existing regulatory requirements. In particular it appears to run counter to what had been understood as a defined, integrated and largely closed system designed for particular product(s), produced by a particular company at a given time and place. It has been and continues to be a common practice that companies that produce halal can utilise their existing brand names for halal purposes or develop new logos to cover their products and services if they so wish. The brand constructed on this basis has no need for and should not be required to undergo separate approval other than to clarify its processes, and how it will utilise the brand itself as a promotional tool in the media. The actual logo applied to the product itself does not have to undergo further investigation; there should be no objection to it from a halal perspective.

Fitting the Halal Paradigm

One of the main problems with the MLA brand is that it has been conceived and constructed in a way that simply does not fit into the halal paradigm. If the MLA conception remains or is perceived to be radically different from traditional practice and from textual guidance or prescription then its legitimacy as a halal brand will be called into question. As a consequence halal consumers' confidence in the brand will be seriously undermined. If the brand is going to make claims other than those that are normally approved and validated through certification, for example to influence purchasing behaviour of customers, then MLA needs to consider the status of those claims in the halal context and following that validate them through a competent authority. Muslims would need to know what halal is being associated with and what assertions are being made about it and how it is being used and represented. This would be the case for example in product advertising where a company may assert any number of claims for its products that are outside the scope traditional product certification. If the values expressed in the representation or rendering of a halal product or a halal brand contains references or imputations that are inconsistent with or divert from halal norms and values then its halal claims will be contested vigorously. Further, its credibility may be severely damaged.

The Parameters of Halal Certification

One of the most important principles in halal rules and procedures is that they must be in their application verifiable. Verifiability in this sense means that they must be shown upon examination to be in accord with the *Sharia* or compliant in situ under the supervision and monitoring of an approved Islamic entity or personnel. Another equally important principle is that the essential halal claims of products validated by halal certification is only to the extent that the products so certified are fit for consumption by Muslims and other halal consumers and that in particular where slaughter is concerned that they are prepared according to Muslim rites. Separation of halal from haram and non-halal is also a key rule in all aspects of processing, storage and display of halal products. In other words validation is not open ended but is in fact and by legal implication limited to specific criteria based on Islamic norms and standards. In terms of symbolic representation of the brand, halal products and services can not be advertised or rendered in the marketplace in ways that contravene halal standards.

What follows from this is that while the halal system can be applied to one product category of a particular company at a given time and place, in the same way as it is applied to other products produced or manufactured by other companies in other locations, each system's approval and application in a given location nonetheless is deemed *sui generis*. That is to say that each is treated as separate and distinct from those operating in other establishments. That is the reason why each halal establishment belonging to a particular company is required to develop and submit for approval its own halal program. Each is designed to stand independently on its own without reliance on, reference to, and transference to or from the other establishments. The brand therefore being a wholly independent entity and possessing a distinct corporate personality of its own can in no way rely or assume characteristics which itself does not posses, functions it does not perform and standards it does not have on the basis that others with which it is closely associated or represents have legitimately acquired them and on this basis argue that it should be able to use the halal symbol on their behalf. But as pointed out above it is not possible to aggregate halal products in this way without making the case to relevant authorities in the first instance and without getting their approval. Another way of expressing the distinctiveness of the product based halal certification system operating in each halal registered enterprise is to say that it is a micro-system of compliance which is an integral part of a universal halal system based on the *Sharia*. It cannot be fashioned to suit MLA brand imperatives but in fact the reverse: the MLA brand must be designed to meet halal imperatives.

MLA is not the only western corporation or enterprise that has utilised the halal concept for commercial purposes. But the way it has obtained halal approval- if indeed it has- and how it wants to utilise it is entirely different from any other major corporation. For the overwhelming majority of enterprises the utilisation of halal is to have their products- products they produce, manufacture own or export- obtain halal status, by complying with appropriate standards and regulatory requirements based on the *Sharia*. The MLA is not in the category of enterprises that do this; nor is it in the category of enterprises characterised as corporate brands that utilise halal for a small component of their product profile from time to time to target a particular segment of the global Muslim market. These corporations use their own brand on their label and if need be an additional halal inscription showing the status of the product as a halal product. What is obvious about the MLA brand is that it is typologically different from the brands referred to above. It is also clearly different in the sense that not only does it not have any products of its own to sell, but its brand has not applied appropriately for halal status, whatever the basis for its application might ultimately be. On the presumption that MLA will utilise the halal brand for marketing purposes alone, it is difficult to say whether it will obtain legitimate halal approval. What can be said with certainty is that halal approval is and indeed ought to be dependent on the extent to which MLA's brand complex meets halal standards. However, it is abundantly clear that there are legal and other *Sharia* issues that need to be sorted out before any halal approval is granted to the MLA brand. Above all the project needs to be legitimised and given credibility. It currently lacks both.

There are serious difficulties associated with MLA brand from a halal perspective, not least of which is its distant association with and claims to symbolic representation of too many halal products and enterprises. They do not stem so much from the assertion that it is a brand *per se* as they do from what kind of brand or symbol it is- in terms of its functions, characteristics, standards, methods and means of operation- and how it fits into the halal paradigm. What is most unclear for example is how this unique brand is going to be rendered in halal markets as well as globally. So wrapped in mystery is the whole project that there is no information available about it in the public domain. For the MLA this may have seemed the easiest road to construct its brand idea, but the easiest road may prove the most treacherous. The type of corporation it is, the goods it produces how it produces them and renders them in the marketplace will have considerable bearing on whether halal approval is likely to be granted and if granted what criteria it would have to meet in order to maintain its halal status. If the corporation seeking approval is a brand corporation, it would require a different program and a different set of criteria from a corporation like MLA where the symbol is utilised merely to represent the products of corporation members- as seems to be the case in this instance. The effect of MLA's brand project is to add another layer of halal approval to existing certification by an entity removed from both ownership and production. Direct relationship of the brand with branded products is an important criterion for halal credibility and accountability. The more removed an entity is from ownership and production, the more removed its responsibilities are for halal status and halal certification of products.

A Clearer Path to Halal Status

The Key question in the first instance is not so much whether the products MLA represents in its brand complex are halal or halal certified important though that is, rather what the halal credentials of MLA are, and what is its relationship with these products in terms of production, manufacturing, ownership and control. There is in fact nothing wrong with the commercialisation of halal, nor specifically with its utilisation as part of a brand complex. To do so, however, the supremacy of halal must always be paramount and shown to be paramount. That is to say that its application ought to be in compliance with halal norms and standards. It can not be otherwise. It is not easy in Islam to justify halal status if these issues are obscure or remain unclear and in particular if a direct relationship with a halal product or service can not be clearly established. It seems inappropriate to characterise a brand as halal without actually knowing the criteria on which this claim is made and without MLA submitting as a matter of course a halal program, as part of its application to a competent authority, on the basis of which halal approval is either granted or denied. A competent authority in the current circumstances can not be Australian halal certifiers whose jurisdiction remains limited to single product certification, and for the overwhelming majority of certifiers only meat certification. At the very least MLA would need to have a clear basis for its claim to halal status which on the basis of the above considerations it does not currently have. If it were to submit an application to a competent organisation, the following would be some of the questions it may be required to answer:

- What activities does MLA engage in and what products or services does it trade in?
- How does MLA propose to represent its halal brand in the marketplace?
- Does MLA produce or is MLA involved in the production of any haram or non-halal goods and services and if so in what way?
- Is it involved in any form of assessment, monitoring or supervision of whether halal standards are being met by members or not?

- How does MLA ensure separation of halal from non-halal or haram in regard to the production activities of its members that produce or export halal meat?
- If MLA members include enterprises that produce halal and those that do not, how would the application of halal brand be determined?
- How many establishments/companies does MLA brand cover and at which locations?
- What uses does MLA want to make of a halal brand and for what purpose?
- What products will be branded, how will the halal brand be applied to products or services and at what stage will they be branded?
- How will the use and application of the halal brand be controlled?
- What control does MLA have over branded products and does it have any legal responsibilities to the consumer?
- What are the norms and standards the producers will be required to comply with in order to utilise the halal brand?
- Does MLA have a halal program that sets out the operation and utilisation of the brand and is the program approved by a competent authority?

Responses to these and other questions should be part of a comprehensive halal Program which if approved by a competent halal authority, ought to be audited for compliance from time to time.

There are legitimate ways MLA can validate its halal brand. Before it embarks on this undertaking however MLA must in the first instance accept the necessity of and the need for halal approval for its brand project by a competent authority or a representative designated for this task. Equally importantly, it must recognise that it is not possible to transfer traditional certification of meat to cover purely brand activities. One of the main difficulties in having the brand approved is that there is no model in Australia which can serve as a guide. However there are clear *Sharia* rules and principles that can be applied and by means of which the brand can be validated as halal. The problem is that the overwhelming majority of halal certifiers may not be able to assist in this process because their experience and knowledge is limited to a narrow conception of halal meat certification. A few however may be able to do so, as may individuals with sufficient knowledge or experience of halal norms and standards and particularly how they can be applied to brand or brand based projects. There are four key basic conditions that an entity like MLA must satisfy to claim to be a halal brand.

1. It must be named and given identity as a halal brand within halal norms and values
2. It must be registered and be validated by a competent authority or its representative as a legitimate halal brand
3. It must have an approved halal program
4. It must reaffirm its halal identity and renew its registration from time to time

Accepting the necessity of halal approval means that MLA must also identify the appropriate authority or authorities from whom it would seek halal approval. This would depend on both the scope and objectives of the brand. If it is a global brand then perhaps approval can be obtained from most if not all the major halal authorities- Saudi Arabia, UAE, Indonesia and Malaysia. In some circumstances, it may be possible to rely on one or two major halal authorities with sufficient global market reach and influence. The Muslim World league which currently represents Saudi Arabia in halal matters and has offices in more than fifty countries around the world may be a suitable organisation for this purpose.

Conclusion

A fundamental flaw in the construction of the MLA brand stems from its failure to make a clear distinction between product certification and approval of a halal brand. To have made this distinction would have enabled it to recognise that it is not possible to transfer specific product certification to validate a global halal brand neither in its symbolic form nor in its marketing activities. Another major flaw stems from the likely presumption that halal certifiers in Australia can independently validate it and that their acquiescence to the relevant deliberation of the halal consultative committee under AQIS is sufficient for this purpose. Halal certifiers have neither the authority nor arguably the competence to do so at present. Halal certifiers can however play a key role. They can work closely with the MLA, represent the brand to authorities for approval, guide the project to its realisation and ensure that the halal brand is constructed on a sound bases according to *Sharia* requirements. Whatever mistakes that were made in the past can be easily resolved. What is required above all is to refocus the project, give it a distinct halal identity and fit it appropriately into a halal paradigm and following that monitor brand activities to maintain its legitimacy and credibility.

Chapter 4

Thinking Halal, Doing Halal: A Frame of Reference

Introduction

International demand for and interest in halal products and services has increased significantly in the last three decade or so. The global market value of trade in halal food products alone is estimated to be worth more than $580 annually (Hamid 2008) and the combined of Halal food and non-food Halal products is estimated to be more than $2 trillion (Halal Research Council 2006). It is also further estimated by some that the global halal market is growing annually at a rate of 20 to 30% (Soesilowati 2010) and by others to be currently growing at 17 percent (Agriculture and Agri-Food Canada). While halal trade by western countries is steadily growing, this has not been accompanied by a corresponding increase in understanding of what halal is, what its sources are, what principles it is based on, what are its norms and standards and how effectively it can be applied, validated and given credibility. This essay, together with other essays in this book, addresses some of these basic questions. Its aims are twofold: (1) to provide a frame of reference for understanding the concept and the principles associated with it and their foundations and (2) to facilitate better understanding of the concept and its applications on their own terms. It also offers a critique of current halal practices both by firms that produce halal products and halal certifiers that validate these practices.

Basic Misconception of Halal

Halal is a composite term used to designate the most important component of a set of interrelated fundamental principles, norms and values based on Muslim law- the *Sharia*. The rules regarding halal are not well understood nor fully appreciated, by many western firms – and some of their Muslim counterparts- that want to utilise it for the production, sale and marketing of goods and services. In their application to food for example many halal producers and exporters apprehend it as a concept that is akin or equivalent to consumer satisfaction based on varied product specifications demanded by Muslim countries or customers. This is not totally unrelated to halal rules but is far removed from what halal is and represents.

In part this conception stems from the fact that the term halal to western enterprises is relatively novel and comes from unfamiliar cultural milieu. It can be argued that it gives rise to a hybrid understanding at once seemingly proximate and different from consumer satisfaction: proximate that is in the outward resemblance of the two terms or some of the characteristics they share, and different in the norms and values they embody. It is a perspective that in effect simplifies the concept and makes it immediately accessible and/or explicable but also at the same time obscures the cultural codes that mediate its meaning and comprehension. This rendering is by no means unique, or surprising, in trying to negotiate an unfamiliar or difficult cultural territory. In such circumstance it is not unreasonable to expect western firms to approach the unfamiliar concept from the perspective of another proximate concept with which by tradition, practice and training they are well acquainted or have sufficient mastery of- and particularly one as in this case that has a long tradition in market theory of customer satisfaction.

The aim of firms is certainly neither to confound nor to replace the one with the other but rather to apprehend halal, in terms of the broad characteristics of customer satisfaction so that the former becomes explicable. Functionally, what this does is at once to enhance its portability and usability such that it lends itself to deployment with sufficient degree of confidence in the halal specific circumstances. But the extent to which this rendering can assist in reaching an adequate understanding and appreciation of the nature of halal and haram is a different question. In this context it may perform, and satisfy meeting purely technical and procedural functions, but it can hardly be a substitute for proper understanding of halal principles and can in fact result in misapplication of its rules, as demonstrated most graphically in the report on the halal registered establishment contained in this book. There is therefore need for business to better comprehend what halal means, what its rules are, what value is placed upon its application by halal customers and how it can be rendered most appropriately in the marketplace. To do so, it is imperative for business to understand the concept in its own terms. The effect of this will be not only to maintain the ethos and integrity of the concept but also enhance the capacity of business to maximise their opportunities in the global halal market.

Understanding Halal on its Own Terms

The tendency of some enterprises to utilise a substitute for halal in the above manner, in effect simplifies the concept but at the same time carries the risk of seriously compromising it. While Muslims accept the market principle of customer satisfaction it is nonetheless solely understood in the sense that it is subsidiary to and must operate in the framework of the halal principle. The one is a divine rule compliance with which is obligatory and satisfies God, the other is a rule of the material world for the satisfaction of the needs of men and women. The two principles are by no means mutually exclusive from an Islamic perspective. Firstly the material world is merely an extension of the spiritual realm. Secondly, not only are they interdependent but the actions in the former are consequential in the latter. In Islam only if the customer satisfaction is in conformity with the halal rules does it have spiritual merit and befits to be characterised as halal. Otherwise it would be outside the scope of halal norms and standards. Depending on the nature of products and services in question and how they are manufactured or represented, customer satisfaction can be halal or haram or any of the other grades in between. The test is whether the concept as applied, complies with halal rules and standards and whether the methods used for this test are credible. If for example a product is non-halal or haram (prohibited), then customer satisfaction does not apply, as Muslims are not allowed to utilise or consume it. If on the contrary however the product is halal then customer satisfaction is highly valued and is applied in the same way as any other customer would irrespective if he or she is Muslim or non-Muslim.

In understanding halal a different mindset is required. That mindset is one where halal values are preeminent in the operation of business and the standards it should meet for validation of the goods and services produced or traded. The implication of this is that halal must be understood in its own terms rather than in terms of other postulates and assumptions. This approach would have significant advantages for business: (1) it would lead to a better understanding of halal and therefore to better application of and compliance with its halal norms and standards. (2) improve the ability of firms to adapt successfully to halal rules and regulations (3) strengthen and broaden the ethical foundations of business (4) increase and strengthen the level of uniformity of halal standards as a system and (5) potentially unlock a huge untapped global market in halal products and services.

One of the major barriers to understanding halal is to view Islam and its precepts as purely transcendental and therefore otherworldly. In very important respects Islam is also about the material world and how human beings can best adapt to, make sense of and interact in it and at the same time prepare themselves for the hereafter. Halal is therefore grounded in practice and so too is religion of which it is part. In other words worship alone (relationship with God) is not sufficient for personal development and salvation, conduct (relationship with your fellow human beings and interaction with the natural environment) are equally important. Halal and haram are the fundamental concepts in Islam that define, regulate and guide the conduct of human affairs.

Halal and Haram as Divinely Ordained Principles

There are no concepts more fundamental to Islamic thought and practice than halal (permitted) and haram (prohibited). Together with other associated concepts of which they are part they have their roots in Islamic law. The ethical doctrine in Islam is intimately connected with the law. Both the rules regarding conduct and relationship (*Mua'malat*) and those regarding ritual worship (*Ibadat*) are an integral part of one another and form part of a practical code which Muslims live by in their daily thoughts and actions. The term *Sharia* in Arabic means the path, and is used by Muslims to broadly designate Islamic law. Islamic law is comprehensive and is defined by Muslim scholars as "the body of those institutions which Allah has ordained in full or in essence to guide the individual in his relationship to God, his fellow Muslims, his fellow men and the rest of the universe" (Abd Al Ati 1977).

The *Sharia* is based on divinely ordained rules and pronouncements contained in the Quran (The Holy Book of Islam) and the Sunna (traditions of the Prophet Mohamed). Together they constitute the primary sources of Islamic law and contain the principles upon which it was developed and ultimately systematised. This process culminated in the four schools of Muslim law which though they have differences in interpretation and emphases on a small number of matters nonetheless are from the same sources and have a uniform outlook that complement each other. That body of law which was developed as a science into Islamic jurisprudence is designated as *Fiqh*. The term *fiqh* literally denotes intelligence or knowledge. "It does not designate the principal Islamic laws that are to regulate all aspects of public and private life; rather it is a subsidiary [albeit an essential] science of those laws"(Abd Al Ati 1977). The *fiqh* in a very important sense is the exposition, interpretation and application of the primary sources and incorporates the methods and means of reaching pertinent conclusions on matters of law and morality. Those matters that concern ritual and those regarding conduct are not only an integral part of each other but they are consequential if not in the here and now but inescapably in the hereafter. Although in common parlance the *Sharia* and *fiqh* are used synonymously, analytically they are not the same. Muslims may speak of or refer to different schools of law (*Madahib* plural, *Madhab* singular); they do not speak of the *Sharia* in the same way (Abd Al Ati 1977). The distinction is simply this: the *Sharia* is primary source of law, divine in origin, religious in essence and comprehensive in scope. The *fiqh* by contrast is the product of human intellect to systematise, interpret and apply the *Sharia*. However the *Sharia* is most commonly used to designate both the principles embedded in the primary sources as well as the secondary and subsidiary sources including the *fiqh*. This combination explains the nature and conception of Islamic law as both divinely ordained and socially grounded.

Halal (or Permissibility) as a First Order Principle

In Islam the original state of man is liberty and the first principal pertaining to him in the material world is by the grace of God permissibility. But it also recognises that the exigencies of social life must compel its limitation. What this means is that the things God has created are in the first instance essentially for the use and benefit of human beings and are therefore permissible or halal. A corollary of that is nothing is prohibited or haram unless specifically designated as such by an explicit verse in the Quran or a sound Hadith of the Prophet (Peace be upon him (PBUH)). There are many verses in the Quran which underscore God's bounty and blessing on humankind, among them the following:

> It is He who hath created for you all things that are on earth ... (2:29)

> And He has subjected to you, as from Him, all that is in the heavens and all that is on the earth: behold, in that there are signs indeed for those who reflect. (45:13)

> ...He has subjected to your (use) all things in the heavens and on earth; and has made His bounties flow to you in exceeding measure, (both) apparent and unseen. (31:20)

The term halal is that which is permitted in Islamic law; conversely haram is that which is prohibited. By comparison with the vast, almost infinite scope of things God has permitted mankind, there are only a few things He has prohibited. The principle of natural permissibility or liberty inherent in halal therefore gives human beings the widest scope of freedom in what they may consume, utilise or do. Haram, by contrast is limited in its scope to a small number of objects and a narrow sphere of human conduct and behaviour. From this Islamic jurists have reached a twofold conclusion: (1) Liberty finds its limit in its very nature, because liberty unlimited would mean self-destruction- and that limit or boundary is the legal norm, or law and (2) No limit is arbitrary, because it is determined by its utility or the greatest good of the individual or of society. Utility, which is the foundation of law, traces also its boundary and extent (Grunebaum 1953).

The categories of things that are haram are made explicit and sometimes the reasons are given as to their prohibition. Prominent among them is that they are impure, cause or have the potential to cause harm or likely to undermine the personal and spiritual integrity of the individual as a member of society. It follows from this that the rules regarding halal and haram are neither arbitrary nor purely transcendental, but are based on sound social principles: that of utility and human welfare. On the measure of human welfare alone a product or an activity is haram if it has manifest harmful impact on the wellbeing of an individual or on society as a whole. The grounds for prohibition may in some cases be immediately apparent or understood by reason of their effect, as in the case of drugs and alcohol, because of the immense harm they can cause. However there are instances in which the limits of human reason and the stage of scientific development may not always expose the wisdom of a particular prohibition. And in such circumstances, as indeed in others, there is no more fitting and reliable basis for trust than in that which God has ordained.

Two of the most outstanding characteristics of halal are the inherent notions of the wellbeing of human beings and the vast scope of things it covers both of which by God's grace and mercy enable mankind to derive the maximum benefit from his environment. Wellbeing is at the heart of the concept such that halal is often defined as that which is good, wholesome, beneficial and pure; whereas haram is defined as its opposite: that which is harmful and impure. The Quran states:

> They ask thee what is lawful to them (as food). Say: Lawful unto you are (all) things good and pure... (5:5).

This day (all) things good and pure are made lawful unto you.... (5:6) and further says: Eat of the good things we have provided for your sustenance, but commit no excess therein. (20:81)

Prevention of harm is itself therefore a necessary part of maximising human wellbeing and welfare. To underscore their marked difference, the rule in relation to these contrasting concepts was put by Sheikh Al Qardawi thus: "If something is entirely harmful it is haram, and if it is entirely beneficial it is halal, but if its harm outweighs its benefit then it is haram." This principle derives from the following concrete example in the Quran:

They ask thee concerning wine and gambling. Say (O Prophet): In them there is great sin or [harm] and some benefit for human beings, but the sin is far greater than the benefit... (2:219).

Towards an Operational Definition of Halal

Halal is a positive concept based as we have discussed on permissibility and liberty with qualities of goodness, wholesomeness and wellbeing as important components implicit in its meaning. However, it is not easy to define halal on its own for at least two reasons; firstly, it does not have an independent existence except in relation to its opposite and other associated concepts and; secondly the scope it covers is so wide and so extensive to narrow it down to defined limits. Furthermore, to say that halal is that which is permitted in Islamic law is simply to say the same thing. Hence it is not a clear and detailed definition that tells us what it is but a tautology that hardly explains its meaning. Perhaps the best way to define halal is to do so negatively by way of its opposite and saying that which it is not. Thus in the first instance the definition of halal may be rendered as the absence, exclusion or prevention of haram and doubtful (*Mashbooh*) things, with haram being those things (conduct, products, services etc.) that are prohibited by an explicit Quranic injunction or a sound Hadith or Sunna of the Prophet Mohammad (PBUH). A less rigorous and broader alternative rendition of halal is that which according to the *Sharia* is considered wholesome good and beneficial for mankind but free from haram contaminants. This would however require further definition of both haram and contaminants. The limits of the law in extremis is defined by way of prohibition, hence the whole focus of that which is permissible is the prevention of haram- the limit that humans must not transgress. The overwhelming majority of the things that are prohibited in meat and meat preparation are contained in this Quranic verse.

> Forbidden to you are the flesh of dead animals and blood and the flesh of swine, and that which has been dedicated to any other than Allah, and that which has been killed by strangling or by beating or by falling or by being gored, and that which has been (partly) eaten by a wild beast except that which you make lawful by slaughtering (before its death) and that which has been sacrificed to idols…(5:4 (5:3))

While on the one hand it is generally acceptable among Muslims to define halal negatively in the above manner, as the absence or prevention of haram or *Mashbooh*, on the other hand the concept of haram may be defined similarly as the absence of halal, but is not commonly done so. The concept of haram can be more adequately defined because of the limited scope of things it covers, whereas halal does not similarly lend itself to be as easily defined because of the vast scope of things it covers. That is why halal rules and standards are substantively about the prevention or exclusion of haram or the practices and norms that can lead to it or create the conditions for it to occur. Even the most independent and specific component of halal, that of blessing an animal prior to slaughter by invoking God's name as a fundamental legitimising and validating ethic, is performed at least in part as a mandatory ritual to prevent the animal being sacrificed unto false gods which is of course haram. This has particular significance for abattoirs that slaughter large numbers of animals for sale in Muslim markets. Blessing the animal in this way is the most important step to obtaining halal status. Failure to do so simply renders it haram.

Associated Principles:

There are other associated conceptual categories fundamental to Islamic law. Some follow from and are a logical extension of halal and haram and others fall into different but corresponding classifications. As a logical extension not only is haram prohibited anything that leads to it or knowingly encourages its occurrence or utilisation is also haram. Furthermore things that are designated halal can not be prohibited or made haram and vice versa; things that are haram can under no circumstances be made halal, unless dictated by necessity. In clear direct reference to those who deny themselves or prohibit the pleasures God has permitted the Quranic verse says:

> Ye who believe! Do not make haram the good things which Allah has made halal for you, and do not transgress; indeed Allah does not like transgressors. And eat of what Allah has provided for you, lawful and good and fear Allah, in whom you are believers (Al Quran 5:90-91; 87-88 in Al Qardawi)

The prohibition of haram is absolute and irreversible. It must be stringently applied and observed by all those engaged in halal trade and commerce. Halal norms and standards that are applied in practice are about both validating the halal status of the goods and services in question as they are about confirming the prevention and exclusion of haram in making and processing them. Apart from halal and haram there are other associated concepts relevant to business in the production and sale of goods and services. Of particular significance are the concepts of *Mashbooh* and *Makrooh*. *Mashbooh* means doubtful in terms of its classification as a category in relation to halal or haram. It refers in particular to those cases where it is unclear whether a product or activity is halal or haram and its status is dubious in the circumstances and can not therefore be determined. In such circumstances, Islam advises Muslims to avoid altogether that which is *Mashbooh*, first as an act of piety, second as away of avoiding that which can potentially be haram and third, as an opportunity to further explore and ascertain its real status. In relation to this principle the Prophet (PBUH) has explained it in this way:

> The halal is clear and the haram is clear. Between the two there are doubtful matters concerning which people do not know whether they are halal or haram. One who avoids them in order to safeguards his religion and his honour is safe, while if someone who engages in a part of them

he may be doing something haram... (quoted in Qardawi undated).

A different but associated category is that of *Makrooh* which means that which is disapproved, hated or disliked. The concept refers to certain class of actions or substances that are deemed, in relative terms distasteful and are therefore disapproved, but nonetheless are legally permissible. They are neither prohibited nor fully approved with the implication that they depend on the conscience of the individual. It is not often easy to be definitive about which actions or substances fall into this category in relation to business but any actions that have the potential to lead to anti-social behaviour, exploitative, and uncompetitive conduct or lead to the committal of haram acts for example smoking, may fall under this category. And so too would the denial or obstruction of others the freedom to act in their own positive self interest within the limits of that which is permissible. Among the substances one writer identifies as *Makrooh* are those that cause "drug dependency and smoking substances" (Hussaini 1993). But the examples he offers may be argued by other Muslims to constitute not merely Makrooh but in fact haram. The relevance for business is that while it is obvious that prohibition of haram is categorical, *Makrooh* should be regarded as an inappropriate conduct for business to engage in or accommodate. The important point to make is that there is no legal impediment to engage in practices that are merely *Makrooh*, however much they may be undesirable. In the social sphere, divorce is categorically *Makrooh*, but there are no penalties or prohibition against it, even though it is said to be one of the most hated acts in the eyes of God.

Intimately associated with the principle of permissibility and other related principles is that of universality. These principles are first and foremost universal because they are decreed by God for the benefit and wellbeing of mankind. They allow no exemption based on status, nationality, creed or colour or indeed any other distinctions. They are therefore obligatory and binding on all human beings to comply with. No earthly power has the authority to change or modify halal rules and standards, even where permissibility is paramount. In effect they are removed from human jurisdiction- except where arguably in rare circumstances there are clear differences among the schools of law. A pertinent corollary is that it is incumbent upon Muslim to comply with and maintain, develop and promote the universality as well as the uniformity of halal norms and standards.

Uniformity of and Differences in Halal Standards

In the context of the *Sharia*, uniformity of halal norms and standards is an essential requirement. It is however a requirement that does not totally exclude but in practice allows for minor variations. It is therefore misleading to assume complete uniformity in practice even if one may do so in theory. However this does not relate to fundamental principles which remain unchanged, but is consistent with the Islamic tradition of accommodating minor differences in interpretation on a particular matter among some of the four schools of law. This may also extend to the issuance of a *fatwa* (legal opinion) by ulemas in a particular country to clarify the position of the *Sharia* on a specific issue regarding halal or resolve differences that may have arisen in relation to it. In the latter case the fatwa may not be universally endorsed in the manner in which it was interpreted, and apply only to certain countries or communities and not to others. Such determinations may also be a product of tradition and change. An example that readily comes to mind is non-stun meat and the insistence by certain communities and commercial enterprises that it is the only meat they will accept as purely halal- thus rigidly asserting the validity of the traditional norms of halal slaughter. It is an important example because meat products comprise the biggest volume and highest value of halal exports by western countries to Muslim markets. Their opposition in particular is to the consumption of meat where the animal has undergone a stun procedure prior to slaughter. This is not limited to some Muslims; certain Jewish communities also prohibit eating the meat of animals subjected to stunning as being non-*Kosher*- unfit for consumption according to Jewish law.

Judging from the way they have maintained their position on this issue over the years both ideologically and commercially, non-stun or stun free advocates have a strong following in Muslim countries. Even though they have generally tolerated its importation, they have not sought a ban on meat produced under the stun procedure. However, the overwhelming majority either has no objection to or is in favour of stun prior to slaughter in relation to those imports. Major halal importing countries endorse this procedure, with restrictions on the type of stun and voltage that can be applied. Stunning is a relatively modern technological development. Its use in the slaughter process has not been embraced in nor taken up by Muslim countries where stun free slaughter remains the norm and standard practice. This underpins the strength of stun free advocates. They have retained their commitment to traditional practice whereas those in favour of or have no objection to stun for use in imports from non-Muslim countries have changed by conceding that stun is a legitimate practice in the *Sharia* as part of slaughter process. This represents the dynamic perspective of the *Sharia* and how in particular its principles are re-examined with a view to accommodating new technological developments.

The opposition to stun is due at least in part to a strictly literalist reading of what slaughter connotes in the *Sharia*, what the effect of stun is and to what extent it constitutes an unacceptable innovation (*bida'*). Some would contend that at the very least it introduces doubt (*Mashbooh*) as a category, and in so far as it does it is preferable to avoid it altogether. They would further contend that the potential for the stun to kill the animal before slaughter and hence render it haram in the process is a good enough reason to do so. Lessening the pain of the animal in this process is an important consideration for advocates of both stun and stun free slaughter. The differences are unlikely to be resolved in the short to medium term, with stun free slaughter continuing to be a very small proportion of overall halal meat exports from western countries. In Australia a few abattoirs are given a special dispensation by the government to produce and export stun free halal and *Kosher* meat. In relation to Muslims, the demand for this comes from commercial enterprises that cater exclusively for consumers in Muslim countries who are strong advocates of stun free slaughter.

There are other areas where differences may not be as prominent but are nonetheless important in that business enterprises would need to know precisely what the relevant halal standards to be complied with are. For example such differences may arise from the amount of alcohol present in soft drinks and natural juices. According to the Standardisation and Methodology Organisation for the Gulf

Cooperation Council (GCC) countries residual alcohol should not exceed 1 per cent for grape vinegar and .5 for other vinegars. The standard specifies 0.5 percent to be the maximum limit in apple and grape juices and 0.3 percent as the maximum limit in mango and lemon juices (Al Katheeri 1996). It is possible that this interpretation is not universally accepted; nevertheless it shows a national or a regional approach by governments to *Sharia* based regulations and the possible differences to which it can give rise. For Muslims the presence of any amount of alcohol that is added in food is haram; the residual component refers to the amount that may occur only naturally. The specification of 0.5 percent alcohol as the maximum allowable in the case of soft drinks is not different from European and U.S. guidelines, which is basically the level for non-alcoholic drinks. In a speech to a halal conference in September 1996, the Director of Majelis Ulama Indonesia (MUI) raised the question of alcohol in food in the following way:

> …we can infer that the essence of that which makes one drunk is Khamar [meaning alcohol] and this includes substances that impair or change the functioning of the mind. The question is then: Is that drink/food halal, if it contains a low amount of alcohol such that it does not make one drunk or change/impair his faculties? Is alcohol halal if it is used as a solvent of the essence since it evaporates in the process of production? According to the Fatwa Commission of MUI the use of alcohol in Indonesia as a solvent is permitted since alcohol is not *Najis* (filth) [?] (Girindra 1996).

Even though there may not be sharp differences between Indonesia and the GCC on the issue of alcohol content, it does at the same time appear that there is no common position either- with the former not being as clear as the latter in terms of precise measurements. Differences such as these, however minor, are nonetheless unhelpful to business. They arise from lack of cooperation of governments in regard to *Sharia* based regulations. There is need therefore for greater uniformity, clarity and consistency in these regulations.

Operating within the Halal System

Nevertheless, halal principles remain valid even if in interpreting them or by way of a fatwa (legal opinion) or the position of a particular school of law differences may emerge. From a Muslim perspective, it is not possible nor is it indeed conceivable that such differences however constitute a departure from the fundamental principles of halal; rather they can only be about what they mean, how they are interpreted and rendered in country specific halal rules and regulations. Contested positions on either side of any debate have the same principles as their starting point, but may reach different conclusions. Accordingly the above example of GCC allowing the specified level of alcohol content in some drinks does not in any way invalidate the principle that alcohol is haram. The reverse however is true: that a Quranic principle can invalidate a rule, an interpretation or an approved procedure by a halal or government authority, if found to be inconsistent with it. The GCC standard relies on this principle too. The GCC standard is based on the following rationale. Firstly the products are in their origin halal (*Asl*) as a soft drinks or fruit juices and secondly the proportion of alcohol in them are negligible compared to the volume of water or natural juice and that it would neither adversely affect the mind nor the body nor is capable of inducing dependence.

The GCC would argue further that beyond the level specified, it clearly recognises that the products referred to above would be haram. This example does not extend to the amount of alcohol present as a solvent in a cleaning agent, because the product is not for consumption and furthermore that it would evaporate as pointed out above by Professor Girindra. One can not say with any degree of confidence that there is universal agreement on the issue of alcohol content in the sense that there are countries that subscribe to this interpretation and others that do not. In the broad sweep of Islamic law however, these differences are minor and their effect negligible, or ought to be. They are nevertheless some of the very few issues in halal on which differences may appear from time to time. In most circumstances there is a striking level of uniformity in halal principles, their interpretation and application. A major exception to this is the differences in halal standards which halal importing countries are required to comply with. Firstly the differences reflect a distinct preoccupation with national specific standards, processes and procedures at the expense of uniform standards; secondly, and following from this a reluctance to subscribe fully to uniform standards and a failure to embrace the original conception of halal as a universal principle. Universality of halal in essence means that there can be no varied conceptions or applications in practice except where they are due to minor interpretations that have their source in schools of law, or justified broadly on grounds of a fatwa but certainly not to serve a purely national agenda or interests.

The halal slaughter of animals and the production of their meat are relatively more straightforward than the production of processed food. Over and above the standards that apply to halal meat there are other issues of greater complexity that pertain to processed food including beverages. The same is true of cosmetics and pharmaceutical products. Most Islamic societies that certify halal therefore refrain from certifying processed food and limit themselves to meat for which they are particularly accredited. Among the most outstanding issues in processed food are the number and type of ingredients, preservatives and other additives that go into the make up of say a particular can of soup, condiment or children's formula and the extent to which they are halal or more specifically halal compliant. Compliance is the means by which halal is validated as having satisfied the requirements of a prescribed standard(s) in this case the specified halal standard or a set of halal standards of halal importing countries. The question in the first instance is, is the product, the ingredients and other additives contained therein halal? Secondly, if they are halal who validated or certified them, how and on whose authority? There is serious concern among some GCC countries about the halal status of many processed foods coming into the market. Their concern was highlighted after discovering misleading and inaccurate product labelling with false or deceptive halal claims. At a conference in Melbourne in September 1996 the Head of the Quality control & Specification Department underlined the seriousness of these problems. He exhibited a wide range of processed products that contained uncertified meat or had ingredients in them, such as gelatin and lard that were clearly haram. In addition to the composition of the products and their lack of authenticity as halal products, he expressed concern about one case in which the halal certificate accompanying a product appeared to have been forged and or incorrectly completed (Al Katheeri 1996).

Role of Governments and other Authorities

In a strict sense neither governments nor religious authorities can legislate on halal and haram. They can only interpret, streamline and systematise the law pertaining to these principles and ensure that they are applied and fully complied with. No Muslim authority would claim otherwise or suggest it alone has the power to make halal laws or in any way override the provisions of the *Sharia*. It follows therefore that the only law that is pertinent to halal and haram is the *Sharia* and any rules procedures and administrative norms and practices must be subsidiary to, be based on and remain consistent with it. In other words such procedures that are adopted are subject for their validity on the extent to which they are in conformity with the *Sharia* principles. Failure to do so invalidates business procedures and practices as well as any supposed halal norms and standards that have been utilised, rendering them noncompliant.

None of this however detracts from the role of authorities and government to uphold, enforce and improve the systemic application of the law in the way it was intended. For business enterprises there are a number of implications that follow from this: (1) Muslim governments and authorities have no power to change or vary halal principles or for that matter endorse halal standards, processes and procedures that are inconsistent with or deviate from *Sharia* sources; (2) Halal rules and procedures must represent the majority legal opinion of Muslim scholars and jurists and, (3) Business enterprises can not negotiate or make representations for the variation of rules based on halal principles with halal certifiers. If in the process of production certain goods are contaminated and rendered haram, then those goods must be disposed of and corrective action taken to ensure that the problem does not recur. In the example given on chapter 7 (the inspection report), where a factory was found to be producing pork (a haram product) in the same premises as halal meat, the only possible solution would be to have haram production completely removed from the premises. The current practices under which the factory operates is contrary to halal norms and standards and should have been deregistered as a halal establishment. This is the only way integrity and credibility of halal standards could have been maintained. Yet despite the seriousness of the issue, the establishment continues to produce halal and haram in the same premises in circumstances in which the risk of contamination is extremely high, with the full knowledge of government and under the auspices of an Islamic society, which certifies its products as halal. It is not good enough for the establishment to rely on strategic management practices that sees halal compliance as a problem-solving exercise rather than approaching it appropriately from the perspective of an ethic that should be complied with. But the main problem in this case is not so much the factory as it is the Islamic society responsible for monitoring and certification which had allowed haram production to take place. Contravention of halal rules is not limited in this case to those who commit the haram act but it also extends to those who have been complicit in that act and have failed to prevent it when they had the ability and indeed the authority to do so.

The most conspicuous manifestation of halal and its norms and values is its application to food and beverages. But there are many new and innovative ways in which business is utilising the halal concept by applying halal standards to the production, processing and sale of goods and services. In recent times it has been increasingly applied to financial products, pharmaceutical products and cosmetics. There are also new attempts being made to utilise it as a marketing tool for brands and branding practices in various ways. Undoubtedly, halal is emerging as a distinct and recognisable concept in the lexicon of international trade and commerce- with a steady and potentially vigorous growth in volume and scope of products and services traded as halal or halal approved. The distinction of halal and halal approved is important. First there are many products and some services that are by their nature (*Asl*) halal and do not need halal approval; secondly there are others that are properly validated by a competent halal authority and are therefore halal approved or halal certified; thirdly there are those that may be or are halal and need halal approval but have not been properly validated by a competent halal authority as halal. In this case, not only do the halal claims lack credibility but the status of goods produced by this means can only be characterised as non-compliant or deficient. Fourthly, there are dubious, unauthorised or simply haram products that fraudulently claim halal status.

Validating Halal

Validation of products as halal is not, as suggested above, always mandatory or a necessary requirement. Where it is not mandatory, halal authorities should not insist on it as a matter of course. This is particularly the case with food and beverages that are halal in origin (*Asl*) and have not been adulterated or contaminated in any way by non-halal or haram products. Examples of these would include water, natural fruit, and grains etc., provided they are unadulterated, are free from *najis* (impurities or filth) and chemical contamination and remain substantially in their natural state. Despite this there have been a number of cases where Islamic societies have approved products as halal when in fact they ought not to have done so in accordance with halal principles. An example which comes to mind is the approval and certification by a major Islamic society in Australia of soccer boots and balls exhibited at a halal conference in October 2007. There was also some reference by a speaker at that conference to certifying tomatoes and potatoes. Many Muslims would view this as utterly inappropriate conduct, one that not only trivialises halal but also demeans it. Such practices go to the heart of what is wrong with the current certification system and highlights the need for reform. The objection here is not so much to the advice and general approval that a company might seek and receive to engender confidence in its product being acceptable to Muslims but the display of an approved halal insignia or label on the product in this way without consideration of its impact on the reputation of halal norms and standards. There should be clear guidelines for business on issues of this kind. The tendency by a few societies to engage in excessive halal labelling and certification is counterproductive and must be restrained to protect the credibility and reputation of halal norms and standards. There is also need to consider who can use the term halal in product labelling in what circumstances and according to what rules. In particular it is important to distinguish between approved halal labelling and unapproved labelling in order to protect customers from products of companies that may be making false or misleading claims. It is imperative that the whole issue of halal labelling be brought under strict control.

While the category of *Asl* products referred to above may not normally require halal validation this may however be necessitated in some circumstances by a number of considerations. Prominent among them would be to draw a clear distinction between purely halal products and similar products in the market that are impure, contaminated by additives and/or carry misleading or deceptive halal inscriptions or labels. In these circumstances the aim of validation is to ensure that the customer is able to distinguish between an authentic halal and an unauthentic or dubious 'halal product'. Validation in this sense is also an instrument for control of halal production which also helps customers distinguish competing halal claims of products in the marketplace. It is important to make the point however that the use of validation in this way is not strictly a *Sharia* based requirement but a purely administrative instrument for the management of halal practices.

Halal Validation is in many ways playing an increasingly prominent role in international trade and commerce. The growth in Halal trade is at least in part stimulated by Muslim customers' demand for halal compliant products and services which has prompted national governments to devise ways of facilitating this demand. This is in a sense a distinctive if not a unique development. Much more than simply a product based demand, it is one based on compliance with an ethic comprising specific religious standards that sustains and defines this demand, without which the product would have little or no customer demand and no markets to trade in the Muslim world. The demand for halal is by no means new and is perhaps as old as the advent of Islam- and Muslims believe that its origins go back to both Christianity and Judaism. Its uniqueness is not simply about the growing halal demand *per se* but about the complex combination global imperatives that drove it, the institutions it forged and the systems it created to foster the development of halal trade and commerce. The present strong growth in demand reflects not only the level of expansion of trade and commerce in this field but also a substantial increase in economic status of Muslim customers throughout the world. The migration and settlement of large Muslim populations in major western halal exporting countries has also stimulated this demand. In response to these demand pressures a few major halal importing Muslim countries have developed regulations and standards with which companies must comply in order to meet importation requirements. These rules and regulations are *Sharia* based standards. They are applied instruments for the control and management of halal in the context of various other national and international regulations and procedures that are operant in various countries in the western world.

The Development of Demand for Halal

These demand pressures not only brought about differing national based halal regulations (Indonesian, Malaysian, Singaporean etc.) but also from the Muslim perspective new institutions that control halal food production- particularly meat products imported from Non-Muslim countries. New institutions or departments within existing institutions with responsibility for halal management and control were established by countries like Malaysia, Indonesia and the UAE that were broadly referred to as halal authorities. Sometimes they were established as part of a department of religious affairs. In Malaysia in particular this department became part of the Prime Minister's office which gave it considerable status and influence. In Indonesia, the halal authority was conceived somewhat differently in that the Majelis Ulama Indonesia- a religious council- assumed that role and in the United Arab Emirates, the authority was vested in the Secretariat of the General Municipality. On the whole only a few countries were active in these developments. What was common to them was that departments of veterinary services played a central and complementary role with health, hygiene and technical issues as their primary responsibility. This combination has played a positive role in the development of the halal system as we know it today.

From a trade perspective the halal authorities would have found it difficult and impractical to administer halal compliance in overseas countries from which halal products were imported from afar. In this role they relied on local Islamic societies in western countries to both monitor compliance and to certify halal exports. In this capacity they acted in effect as agents to monitor, validate and certify products according to each overseas country's specific halal importation requirements. In Australia, until the late 1980s the societies enjoyed a large measure of independence from the overseas halal authorities, (such as Indonesia, Malaysia and Saudi Arabia) and from the relevant Australian government authority AQIS. Over the years however the societies gradually came under a tight and overlapping control by both these organisations (see diagram below). This was a great opportunity to reform these organisations but unfortunately these controls were not accompanied by any measures to improve their performance or lay down strategies for their development. Despite their designation as Islamic societies, it is not always the case they are Islamic societies. In fact they include a significant proportion of privately owned organisations. Even today the fiction that they are Islamic societies remains intact despite evidence to the contrary that many are not.

In order for halal certifiers to represent halal importing countries they ought to have applied for and been granted accreditation by overseas halal authorities. And since there are not many halal accrediting authorities, the few that are granted accreditation to certify for specific countries are used to cover certification for all Muslim countries. It is not clear what halal products they are accredited to certify other than meat products and in fact there is no document from any accrediting country which sets out or defines the scope of their role as halal certifiers. What the criteria are to accredit Islamic societies as certifiers are also generally unknown, presumably because the system may not have reached a stage where it can confidently be transparent. The only criteria that is widely known, which is that the applicant should be an Islamic society is not even applied in practice as pointed out above. Similarly there are no standards against which the performance of societies are evaluated and judged in order to assess their competence, review their registration or to improve the system as a whole. Nevertheless they play a significant role in halal food trade, and are the custodians of the image and reputation of halal in non-Muslim countries. They are the first point of contact for western enterprises to apply for and obtain halal registration and the only means of having their products certified halal for export. Their activities and operations no less their professional and moral integrity in the commercial world shall have implications for how halal is perceived, how it is projected, rendered and transmitted to Muslims and non Muslims alike.

Figure 4 Halal certification system: structure and functions

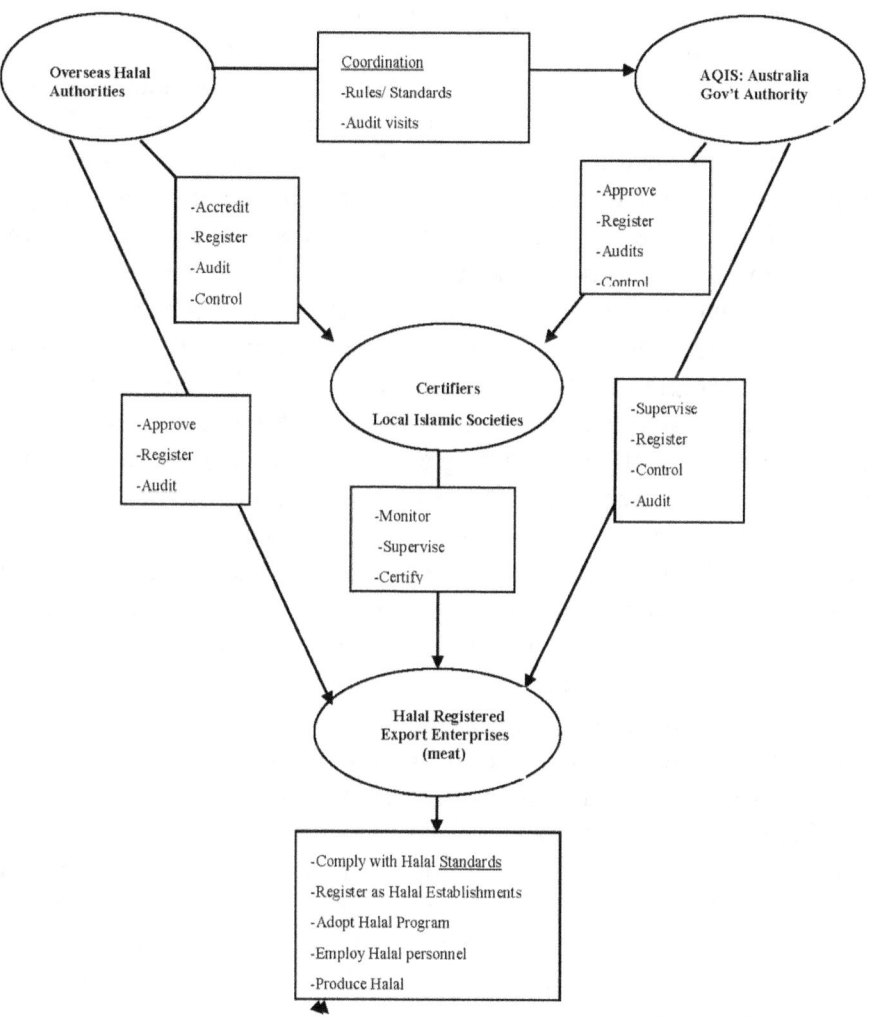

Weaknesses and Strengths of the Halal System

The weaknesses of the current system are many and varied. There is no need however to dwell at length on them except to make the following points. The service provision and management practices of halal certifiers are generally poor. Some rely on outdated methods such as rubberstamping as a primary tool for control, monitoring and certification of halal exports. For the most part halal regulations and procedures remain fragmented, discordant and inconsistent in their application. Worse still there have been no attempts to reform the system and make it more effective, accountable and transparent. A comprehensive reform to deal with these and other weaknesses is long overdue. At present there appears to be no credible effort to stem the tide of deterioration in the integrity and efficacy of halal standards. At the very centre of these weaknesses is that each country deals with its halal issues differently highlighting a purely national preoccupation and perspective. It is therefore no surprise that national based regulations have become entrenched, resulting in lack of cooperation and following from this lack of uniform standards. If Muslims understand anything about halal it is that its standards are uniform and ought to be applied uniformly throughout the world. This runs manifestly counter to that understanding. In the future these problems may well be overcome and in hindsight their negative impact may be seen to have been magnified due to their currency and stage of historical development. Apart from the inconsistent national halal standards, many of the problems of halal certification can be attributed to the prevailing organisational model whose weaknesses though they appear obvious, nonetheless remain unacknowledged or ignored. How they will be viewed in hindsight does not however detract from the fact that there is urgent need for these problems to be resolved. Elsewhere in this book I propose a radically different model for halal certifiers.

Far more prominent and enduring than the weaknesses of the system however are its internal strengths. This is the reason why it has been able to withstand a debilitating regime of inconsistent application of halal rules and regulations. What distinguishes the halal system from other comparable systems is a set of unique and distinguishing characteristics. They are as follows:

(a) the permanence and stability of its principles and rules of operation
(b) the high level of uniformity of its standards
(c) the universality of its principles
(d) the ethical and divine foundations of its standards
(e) the social and welfare foundations of its precepts conceived as that which is good wholesome good and beneficial for mankind
(f) the unobtrusive character of the system and its compatibility and complementarity with most other systems relevant to business enterprises
(g) the relatively low cost of its compliance
(h) the simplicity of adopting its rules and procedures
(i) the global scope of the halal market and its business friendly norms.

This set of characteristics is highly advantageous for business if applied with professionalism and integrity. The problem is that there is a wide and marked difference between the inherent positive characteristics of halal as described above and its operation on the ground- so marked in fact that they at times appear contrary. Throughout its history Islam has encouraged trade and commerce. For example, religious jurisprudence opposes practices that might disturb the free interplay of supply and demand which is allegedly derived from the Prophet's condemnation "of obligatory pricing-fixing, the "maximum", the laying down of price levels by authority." (Rodinson 2007). Halal rules and prohibitions thereof are conceived as necessary instruments through which commerce can be assisted and facilitated. This particular dimension is important because concomitant with the facilitation of free trade there are basic and clear ethical boundaries which commercial enterprises must not transgress.

What is most significant about these characteristics and about halal principles in general is that no temporal power or earthly religious authority has any authority whatsoever to change or modify them. In this sense they are immune from and businesses are permanently insulated from the whims and vagaries of temporal legislative government intervention. They stand solid in their permanence giving business unmatched stability which engenders a strong sense of confidence in the pursuit of trade among nations. In this context they allow for the possibility of national regulatory requirements to be challenged and contested by the public on the basis of their departure or deviations from *Sharia* based halal standards.

It would however be misleading to say that these characteristics and principles can operate in vacuum, or that they are wholly free from the exercise of temporal and religious authority. Indeed they are not. The system is characteristically grounded as other Islamic principles are in social reality of everyday life and its reason d'être is to regulate, guide and give meaning to human conduct. This is what gives it its dynamic nature as well as its relevance. Islamic groups and government have traditionally played a significant role in the operation of and compliance with these halal principles and standards. Without them the system would not work as effectively as it does nor claim to be universal. The role of the human agency in making the system work is not passive but active and highly significant. The success of the system as an effective global standard is largely dependent on the operational capabilities of the certifiers and halal authorities and their professional competence. The more they possess these qualities the better they will be able to contribute significantly to the development of trade and commerce in halal products and services.

Human welfare is a key principle in Islam and halal is the ethical means by which it is utilised and rendered in the economic system. It is for this reason that Islam supports the development of trade and commerce to enable societies to accumulate and distribute wealth in the community. For the same reason it is averse to restrictive practices that distort, or undermine trade unless there are compelling reasons to do so. Businesses would therefore find Islam a receptive and accommodating environment within which they can conduct commercial activities, providing they act ethically.

Chapter 5

Prospects of Branding Halal: A Brunei Initiative

Abstract

Brands have become one of the most potent and visible symbols of the global corporate landscape. A halal corporate brand is conspicuously absent from that landscape. The Sultanate of Brunei has recently embarked on an ambitious project to develop a global halal corporate brand. In this paper the issues arising from the notion of a halal brand are explored. The interface between the concept of a brand and the concept of halal is examined and the potential conflicts and opportunities identified and discussed. The paper explores the various perspectives of the Brunei global halal brand including the likely pitfalls and problems of particular approaches. It also considers ways in which the Brunei global halal initiative can be advanced.

Introduction

Contemporary brands are associated in the public mind with super brand names of global corporations such as Nike and Coke. In today's globalised commercial environment the use of brands is pervasive. Even the number of websites offering companies expert advice on one aspect of branding or another according to one estimate, by a researcher in early 2005, exceeded 100,000 (Danesi 2006). Companies that aspire to make an impact in the global market distinguish themselves from others by their brand name which forms the core their identity. In semiotics brands are signs that link products and customers within an overarching system of cultural meanings. A brand is basically a name given to a product or service in a similar way that a name is given to an individual. Both naming practices are cultural acts that are indispensable to the existence of that which they represent. A person is constituted psychologically and socially by naming. The brand name performs a similar function: it gives the brand a true and distinctive social and cultural existence. "By naming a product, the manufacturer is, in effect, bestowing upon it the same kinds of meanings that are reserved for people. In a basic psychological sense, a product that is named is humanised" (Danesi 2006). In this way it is given a cultural definition and a personal identity.

The relationship of brand and halal has never before been explored in Arabic, Islamic or in western literature. While the literature on brand and branding is extensive that on halal is, from a business perspective, by comparison miniscule. This despite the fact that the Muslim world is overwhelmingly a halal world- a world in which the principles of halal are paramount and deemed obligatory in business, cultural and religious affairs. To what extent can a brand successfully adopt a halal profile or assume a halal identity? Are the two concepts compatible or in conflict? Can they be bonded or coupled culturally and are there circumstances bonding them can be characterised as or seen as akin to equivalence such that Brand=Halal? How can a halal brand be legitimised and given credibility at a global scale and what are the likely obstacles and challenges it would face? This paper explores these issues and the implications of the relationship for the Brunei halal brand.

Halal/Brand Perspectives

Despite their proliferation, brands have not emerged as major corporate halal entities in the global market. Recent Muslim owned brands such as Mecca Cola which are claimed to have grown out of Muslim community resentment against "Coca-Colonisation" (The Economist 2004; Balmer 2006), can not be considered in the context of halal-brand relationship because they do not have a halal profile or identity, nor do they claim to be halal compliant. They therefore lie outside the scope of this article. The question of their relationship is, however, of some relevance and it is this: they are a striking affirmation of the validity and efficacy of the brand paradigm. Not only do they emulate the very brand they set out to compete with, but they also borrow its architecture lock-stock-and-barrel. It follows therefore that commercial imperatives are the main drivers of these ventures more than any widespread Muslim community resentment against "Coca-Colonisation".

The extent of brand association with halal remains limited to an occasional product line by some of the major food companies in their portfolio of regular brand offerings for which prior approval had been obtained from relevant authorities. Though positive in these cases, the association of brand with halal is on the whole discontinuous, tentative, ambivalent and fraught with uncertainty. In effect no major corporate brand has to date adopted the halal concept in to-to, certainly not at a global scale. In part this is understandable because of the inherent religious and operational difficulties involved which are significantly greater for non-Muslims than for Muslims and in part because the identity of halal is embedded in Muslim culture and values. If, as is the case however, major brand names like Nestle, can have specific product lines certified as halal, and others like Coke or Pepsi can dispense completely with the need for halal approval (when arguably they should be required to be halal compliant for sale in Muslim countries), there is no reason in principle why a commercial enterprise irrespective of religious affiliation can not develop its own halal brand, subject to meeting the appropriate halal standards. In fact almost all the halal export companies in Australia, New Zealand and other western countries are owned by non-Muslims. Some have been exporting halal food to Muslim countries for more than thirty years. The Muslim world is not only a halal world; it is also a world in which major super brands have been extremely successful. In fact brands are no less represented or sought after in this world than they are in other comparable regions in the world. Accordingly, at the conceptual level at least, it may well be cogently argued that the two terms are not mutually exclusive. This implied qualification however means that the possibility of contesting this conclusion can not in practice be discounted and may in fact be likely in some circumstances.

Halal in Islam and its Market Potential

Islam is the second largest religion after Christianity and the fastest growing in the world. According to the pew Research Centre the world's Muslim population is expected to increase by about 35 per cent in the next twenty years rising from 1.6 billion in 2010 to 2.2 billion by 2030 (Pew Research Center 2011). This growth forecast represents twice the rate of the non-Muslim population over the next two decades- which is an annual growth of 1.5 for Muslims, compared with 0.7 for non-Muslims. Out of the world's total projected population of 8.3 per cent in 2030, Muslims will make up 26.4 per cent, up from 23 per cent of the estimated 2010 world population of 6.9 billion(Pew Research Center 2011). The strong growth in Muslim population, albeit at a somewhat slower rate than in past, accompanied by rising incomes in major Muslim countries has, among other things, stimulated demand for halal products and services.

According to the Agriculture and Agri-Food Canada, the global halal food market is on the threshold of major developments that hold the promise of rapid and sustained growth. It further states that it accounts for "as much as 12 percent of the global trade in agri-food products which will generate growth opportunities throughout the agi-food industry (Agriculture and Agri-Food Canada 2007). The global halal market for food is estimated to be more than 580 billion. If non-food halal products are included, excluding financial products, then the value of the halal market is estimated at more than $2 trillion. It is further expected that demand for halal products will continue to grow strongly in tandem with the increasing size of the Muslim population with some estimates claiming it will grow by 20 to 30 percent annually (Soesilwati: 2010).

Many reports in the food market focus on food products but increasingly products sold under the Halal label are expanding to cover virtually every agri-product in some Muslim countries (Agriculture and Agri-Food Canada 2007).

These are compelling statistics from a commercial and marketing perspective. For Muslims halal and haram are fundamental to Islamic thought and practice. They encapsulate the practical application of the Islamic belief system giving expression to core cultural and moral imperatives which regulate daily human existence behaviour and conduct (Ayan 2001). As a code of conduct and an ethical value system, they permeate the habits of Muslims, their expectations, their decision making, their work practices, their communication patterns, the organization of their time as well as their business and social relations (Ayan 2001). Halal is simply that which is permitted in Islam; conversely haram is that which is prohibited. Their justifications are not purely transcendental. Rather they are based on considerations of human welfare; hence the conception of halal as that which is wholesome good and beneficial for humankind (Ayan 2001). There are also other gradations of moral categories in between, such as Makrooh signifying that which is reprehensible but falls short of being prohibited. Another important principle is that of necessity which permits a Muslim to consume otherwise haram products under very strict conditions and only "in quantities sufficient to remove the necessity..." (Al Qardawi Undated). Where there is uncertainty or doubt about whether a product or act is halal or haram a Muslim is advised to avoid it. But if the law is silent and no inference can be drawn on its position, then that product or activity under question is halal (permitted) and should under no circumstances be included in the haram (prohibited) category (Al Qardawi Undated). Most people may be familiar with halal in the context of its application to food. Halal is now increasing being applied to other fields including, banking and finance. There is also increasing demand for halal pharmaceutical, cosmetics and personal care products. For western corporations understanding and utlising halal norms would be a valuable tool to maximize their opportunities in the Muslim world. In an important sense it would signify successful adaptation to if not membership of the host country's cultural, social and business landscape. For this to gain currency would require a radical shift in the way western corporations do business in the Muslim world.

Given the magnitude of the Muslim populations alone, a global halal brand is a very attractive proposition. Its absence from global brand landscape is remarkable because, other things being equal, it has a very high potential in terms of unmet consumer demand for brand name products and likely sales outcomes. One country that saw the potential of the concept in recent times and is currently working on its realisation is the Sultanate of Brunei (Sheridan 2007). That it is a relatively small Muslim country by comparison with its more powerful Muslim neighbors- Indonesia and Malaysia- both in size and population may not in itself constitute a major obstacle to and has certainly not discouraged it from embarking on the project. But there are potential risks for Brunei to discount the considerable challenges that either of these countries or groups in them can pose for the brand project. Those challenges can come from a variety of sources and legitimised on the basis of various considerations. How serious they are would depend on the extent to which Muslim neighbouring countries believe their interests in halal matters are being compromised or that their own competing halal alternative programs are being threatened by the Brunei initiative.

The Power of Branding

Branding has become a core activity of capitalist accumulation of wealth. Central to marketing everything that is of value or perceived to be of value, its power lies not only in selling the product, the object of the brand, but also the very idea of it in addition to all the positive attributes and associations it can possibly evoke. It is a symbolic representation of a product for the purpose of maximum consumption and maximum profitability. In meaning and application its parameters are extensive and dynamic and can represent a corporation, a product, or a service, a process or any form of utility. It seeks above all to have the idea of the object embedded in the psyche of consumers and potential consumers transforming them into agents for promotion of the qualities of goodness perceived or real that the product or service embodies. Alinda Wheeler (2003) has pointed out that "products are made in the factory; brands are created in the mind". The desire for the brand is thus normalised: those who have it feel good having it; those who do not, aspire to have it to feel good too and may even feel deprived for not having it. Ultimately consumers as embodiments of the brand are implicated, wittingly or unwittingly in their own seduction to the power of the brand becoming the leading advocates, promoters and exhibitors of the brand and/or the corporation that owns it.

In the brand world a consumer faced with a myriad of alternatives will tend to select that which will give him/her the security, the satisfaction and the certainty of having chosen well- the brand name with which he is familiar and to which he had developed an attachment; a bond. It is not necessary for him to check the price of another product. He will therefore choose say a Nescafe' jar in preference to and perhaps without considering other alternatives. "This" say Parratt and Holloway (1990) "is the power of the brand; Nescafe' having succeeded in excluding competing coffees from consideration by the consumer, does not have to react to competitors who reduce prices by 5 p or offer 10 per cent extra free because the consumer will probably be unaware that such offers are available," or may simply choose not to respond to the possibility of choice. The paradox of this is that while Nescafe' offers the customer one choice among a variety of choices available to him/her, in reality its power is such that it excludes or severely limits other choices. Through this power it is therefore able to create an internationally dispersed club of loyal customers. It reinforces the view that "a brand's substance is not in the product or its packaging, in its name or its manufacture; it is in the mind of the consumer who returns time and again for the product" (Parratt & Holloway, 1990).

Major corporate brands symbolise high status, worth and "excellence" of their enterprises. Accordingly they attract high financial values in excess of their tangible assets. That they can do so is a measure of the success of the brand- a success in which perceptions play a large part. In pure financial terms the importance of brands is clearly shown by the price that companies have been prepared to pay for them. According to Interbrand (c. 1991) in a few brief months in 1988 almost $50 billion was paid for brands in just four deals. Nestle for example paid $4.5 billion to win control of the Rowntree group- more than five times Rowntree's book value. Among the other high profile acquisitions were: the $12.9

billion buyout of Kraft by Phillip Morris, at four times Kraft's tangible assets and, the acquisition by Grand Metropolitan, a U.K. food and drinks company, of Pillsbury for $5.5 billion- a 50 per cent premium on the American firm's pre-paid value and several times the value of its tangible assets. Major brand owners generally acknowledge that the brand is their most valuable and enduring asset. In addition to the above examples, this is reflected in the fact that 59 per cent of Coca-Cola's, 61 per cent of Disney's and 64 per cent of McDonald's capitalization is attributable directly to the value associated with the corporate brand (Balmer 2006). These values are important for our purposes in that they give us an indication of what kind of corporation is being considered by Brunei and the likely scale and significance of its operations.

The Thinking behind the Brunei Halal Brand Project

The power of super brand names and the immense wealth they can generate are key considerations in the Brunei decision to embark on its halal brand initiative. Their overwhelming influence on the thinking of the Brunei government is explicitly acknowledged by its Permanent Secretary of the Ministry of Industry and Primary Resources who is also the Chairman the Brunei Halal Management Committee. He ascribes the decision to launch the Brunei branding project in 2006 to have been "inspired by those well known brands" together with belief that "Halal has the highest potential for brand value and brand loyalty." (Hamid 2008). In order to clarify the power of branding which serves as a model for the Brunei project he offers the following statistics:

According to Interbrand, the brand value of Kellogg's in 2007 was US$ 9.3 billion while Heinz's brand value was US$ 6.4 billion. Compare this to the annual sales by the two companies. In 2006, the global sales of Kellogg's were estimated at US$ 11 billion. In 2007, Heinz's sales globally [were] nearly US$ 9 billion (Hamid 2008).

According to the Brunei government there are compelling economic reasons behind the decision to develop the brand project. And the most compelling is this: the total dependence of Brunei social and economic life on one non-renewable Industry i.e. oil and gas which is unsustainable in the future; hence the need for diversification (Hamid 2008). No other area of commerce could offer a better opportunity for major investment at a global scale and for the prospect of higher returns of the magnitude of corporate brands than a Brunei halal Brand. A project of this kind with a religious underpinning and with an ambitious global scope is bound to generate and bring to the fore consideration of a complex interplay of social, financial, religious and regional political issues. The most prominent among the complex of challenges are: allocating significant financial resources to the project needs and devising and operating a global halal system in which Muslim communities and consumers can have confidence. Brunei has the former in abundance and the latter depends on the planning, future operation and evaluation of the system governing the halal brand.

The expectation of high returns by Brunei from the halal brand are based on a number of considerations set out in the paper presented by the Permanent Secretary of the Ministry of Industry and Primary Resources referred to above. They include:

- The current population of Muslims worldwide estimated at 1.8 billion people
- The global halal market for food and non-food products which may be worth approximately US$ 2.1 trillion annually
- The halal food Industry worldwide with an annual value of approximately US$ 580 billion.
- The projected strong growth of Muslim populations, the improving incomes of Muslims, their changing lifestyles and increasing awareness and understanding of halal
- The increasing demand by Muslims for halal compliant products (Hamid, 2008)

The figures are used here as elsewhere as broad approximations that merely represent expressions of relative magnitude. In that context they may be regarded as no more than indicative of the world Muslim population and the value of global halal food Industry etc. However, it is one thing to recognize the potential consumer demand; it is quite another to realize it. Between recognizing the potential and realizing it lies a complex array of issues which individually or severally will determine the chances of success or failure of the project.

Questions of Ethics, Religion and the Brand

No field of commercial activity or endeavour appears immune from or can entirely resist the incursions of the brand- not even religion. But despite the popularity of branding and proliferation of brands everywhere, it has generated intense debate in various academic, community and consumer circles. The most outstanding has been debates associated with big brand names like Nike in terms of their ethical, environmental and labour practices. More recently there have been technical debates on brand valuation and their credibility. Environmental groups and customers are increasingly concerned about the consequential impacts of products and the externalities involved in their production. They have shown a technically excellent product may not be free from causing environmental damage in production and disposal and have for this and other reasons opposed it (Peattie 2007). Increasingly also they are targeting investors and banks to stop companies undertaking activities that are detrimental to the environment (*The Australian Financial Review* 2003). Due, at least in part, to pressures from communities and environmental groups, one of the major Australian banks has announced its withdrawal from participation in funding the Gunns Pty Ltd Tamar valley pulp mill project, in Tasmania (The Age 2008). An earlier pulp mill project- the Wesley Vale Pulp Mill- was abandoned in the late 1980s due to similar pressures. Other consumer groups have campaigned in favour of rod-and-line tuna or fair-trade coffee and against big brand names in tuna and coffee (*The Australian Financial Review* 2003). In academia conventional dominant marketing assumptions are being challenged by critical enquiry that shows their inherent biases and contradictions, their hidden assumptions and ideological underpinnings.

Muslim countries and communities appear to diverge considerably from this pattern of activism and vigilance in regard to specific brand practices. Social responsibility of corporations has not certainly been a major preoccupation of community groups. They have on the whole been quietist and have shown little or no inclination to contest products and practices that are or likely to have detrimental effects on society or the environment. They have instead uncritically embraced the philosophy and culture of contemporary branding and consumerism as an indispensable accompaniment to corporate success. There is hardly any debate about any specific brand or brands *per se*; their efficacy, value, benefits and impact on society as there has been and continues to be in western countries. Arguably this may reflect the relative weakness, (lack of sophistication or consciousness) of community-based interest groups to challenge dominant commercial and political interests compared to their western counterparts. But while the above proposition may be true in its generality, it can be argued that it is not necessarily true in its specifics. Social and moral responsibility of individuals, groups and business are key principles in Islam. There are Muslim groups in most Muslim countries that wield considerable power and influence even if they are not always in good terms with governing elites. In the extreme, they can appeal to a higher transcendental authority than a mere temporal power in support of their view and for this reason alone governments are disinclined to alienate them. The moral and religious authority they wield is directly relevant to halal and haram in their various contexts. The reference to the quietism of the Muslim communities may not therefore be entirely accurate and may represent a view that does not take fully into account the possibilities for action and the circumstances in which it may arise (Lapidus 1988). The significance of this is that their interests on halal issues are better accommodated than ignored given the potential they have in articulating what these issues are and mediating their outcomes.

That the efficacy of brand, as a marketing activity or as a corporation in its own right, has seldom been questioned in Muslim countries is due at least in part to the fact that branding, in its contemporary form, has rarely if at all been applied to products and processes that ought to be subject to compliance with religious requirements. It had not hitherto manifestly encroached on areas reserved for religious jurisdiction, except perhaps indirectly. Where it has, its encroachment has not been obtrusive or highly visible. In the main it is restricted to seeking accommodation with ethical tenets of Islam and subjecting its products and activities to the rules governing them. This is particularly the case with corporations like Nestle', and Unilever, seeking halal approval for their products. It is possible to argue that given their compliance with religious rules there is no reason to deny them the incorporation of religious or certifying symbols in their brand presentation and hence use them as information and promotional tools for their products by saying in essence they are halal or halal approved.

Contesting Halal Credibility of the Brand: First Order Questions

On the face of it the above are legitimate and valid arguments. If the corporations' products have passed the necessary evaluation of halalness, then there is no justification why they should not be validated as being halal. This is after all the rationale upon which current certification of halal products is based, even though it is possible to draw a distinction between certifying a product line and approving a global halal brand. However, acceptance of this view is contingent upon answers to first order questions. They include among other things: the legitimacy and jurisdiction of the authority on whose behalf halal products are endorsed and the competence of the certifying body conducting the technical and religious evaluation processes as well as the standards and procedures on which validation of the status of the branded products are based. Other fundamental first order questions also include the image and historical profile of the corporation that owns the brand, the content, design and presentation of the brand to the public in the media and public fora. The debate may conceivably raise issues regarding the extent to which a brand serves exclusive or privileged interests and whether those interests are detrimental to or work against the common good of humanity and/or the community. What all this means is that halal branding is a contested field of commercial practice and is likely to be contested more vigorously in the future with the halal brand's emergence into the global commercial landscape .

The scale of the Brunei project is so ambitious that one of the major International marketing and promotion companies Publicis has been commissioned by the Brunei government to develop and operationalise the brand (pers. comm. with key participant, April 2008). (This relationship seems to have been terminated in mid to late 2008). The very scale of the enterprise in its conception, the extensive range of products it might cover, the halal system it will adopt and the evaluation methods it will use render the brand's halal credentials more contested, than would otherwise be the case. To say that basic halal credentials are contested means they inevitably involve serious and legitimate differences about the proper uses that are made of the corporate halal brand, how it is legitimised and evaluated, among other differences that bear on interpretation of rules and standards that pertain to halalness. Any number of interests including governments, Muslim communities, religious authorities, and competitors, Ulemas and secular academics and consumers may raise concerns about one aspects of the brand or another. They may do so by creating doubt in existing norms and practices on the basis of their presumed or real departure from or nonconformity with the norms and standards enshrined in authoritative texts and interpretations thereof. They may also question the rigor and methods with which existing rules and standards are applied. Establishing credibility of the brand means attaining what sociologists would call "closure" by way of removing any substantive doubts that may exist about the products' halal credentials. What this infers is that evaluations of halal, and the determination of their credibility are at least in part political in the sense that they requires arbitration of interests for social credibility to obtain and resolution, or positive realignment of contested positions by those interests to occur.

The validation of halal *per se* has many unresolved problems; the introduction of the brand into these circumstances makes it even more complex. On the one hand existing validation prima facie requires products seeking halal approval to meet control and evaluation standards both religious and technical. On the other hand the standards and control instruments as applied suffer from serious deficiencies irrespective of and without reference to the brand. The most obvious is the lack of uniformity in halal standards worldwide, even though halal as understood by Muslims is a universal system with uniform standards. There are serious contraventions and lax applications of standards as well as, some have argued corrupt practices that also escape scrutiny (Royal Commission Report, 1982). Both the Australian government and overseas halal authorities are aware of these problems. Whatever the justifications are of overseas halal authorities for not addressing these malpractices, the Australian governments attitude appears to be one of "If the system ain't broke, don't fix it" (Australian Parliament 2004). The concern of the Australian government may well be that the whole edifice, weak and ramshackle as it is, may come crashing down if tampered with in the way of reform. There is also no assurance that what it is replaced with will fare any better than the existing structures in terms of competence and educational profile of halal certifying organisations.

Evaluation of Halal and Mediating Group Interests

The concept of a branded product, service or entity that claims to be halal provokes contested positions on a range of issues to which its evaluation is central. Evaluation entails compliance from the point of production to the point of sale to the consumer, with norms and standards that are both technical and religious. It is on the basis of this that halal validation can be obtained. Validation of halal itself is highly dependent on effective and continuous monitoring and evaluation by reliable and competent Muslim personnel. To the extent that monitoring and supervision is weak it increases doubt and reduces halal credibility; to the extent that it is stringent and continuous it decreases doubt and increases halal credibility. The claims to halalness is therefore dependent on the credibility of those that validate it and the acceptance by Muslim consumers, religious and community groups of the integrity of the certifier or the halal authority that legitimises this process. Where both legitimacy and credibility are affirmed through the above processes, the product is for all practical purposes halal and is brand-ready subject to a more general evaluation of the brand itself. Credibility not only refers to socio-religious credibility but what those who carry out the process "know or claim to know" in the context of halal validation. The claim to technical knowledge is not in this sense the only formal property of evaluation, the establishment of a wider network of social-cum-religious and organizational support for practices which can then be routinised and institutionally normalised are equally an important dimension (Power 1992). This perspective represents what might be called the normal/standard conception of evaluation: that is that evaluation entails possession of knowledge by the practitioners of technical and normative standards for validation purposes.

Beyond fundamental injunctions in traditional texts, various interests that may contest halalness in one respect or another are unlikely to have a fixed, uniform view. Interests are dynamic and; their specification is always open to dispute (Hindess 1986). Generally, however, contesting the brand's halal credentials would be largely based on forms of assessments which limit or enable articulation of a particular interest. The appeal to authority (the *Sharia*), questioning of the authenticity of the halal product and claims to the widest constituency will be part of a repertoire of strategies utilised by varying interests to create doubt about or to discredit an existing halal evaluation, standards and practices. Lack of appropriate standards or lax application practices which are not uncommon may attract considerable attention. Interests are also dynamic in the sense that instead of fixed interests and positions adhered to there are varied interests that are formed, reformed and negotiated to achieve new alignments and repositioning of arguments for accommodation and closure by way of rearticulating and repositioning of interests. Arbitration of diverse interests in this way ought to be regarded as normal processes that facilitate and enable consensus to occur or help solidify difference.

The prevailing halal evaluation in Australia deviates considerably from the standard conception in a number of important ways. Firstly, based as it is on different overseas countries' systems, it lacks a universal framework to be applied by a global brand. Other countries systems suffer from similar problems. Secondly, many of those who perform evaluation do not have the requisite knowledge on which the foundation of the standard conception rests. Furthermore, in practice evaluation as a whole is neither a prominent feature nor a necessary requirement in the operation of the current halal monitoring and certification system. An "Audit Report" of halal export establishments developed by the Australian government in the form of a check list is not only an inadequate evaluation instrument but has encouraged malpractices by certifying bodies that seriously undermine evaluation (Copy of Audit Report is with author). It has for example discouraged certifying societies from taking the initiative of an active independent audit of their own, relying instead on passively ticking and signing off on check lists devoid of meaningful evaluation or audit. Muslims would also be averse to any intrusion by non-Muslim entities into areas of Islamic jurisdiction as evident in this case. For these and other reasons a global halal brand can not afford to rely on organisations and systems that do not have the capabilities and the credentials to assist materially in its development. It must therefore consider ways in which it can build alternative standards and systems that are consistent with its global outlook and choose a suitable organisation that can help in that endeavour.

Halal and Brand: Accommodation not a Clash of Concepts

The initiative by the Sultanate of Brunei to develop a corporate global halal brand raises fundamental conceptual, ethical, technical and evaluative issues, among others. The idea of a brand characterised in this way is novel. Because of this the coupling of halal and brand into a single composite category in a global context is likely to attract considerable attention. This is not to suggest that such coupling or integration is ill-conceived or inappropriate. Rather that it is likely to open up a new discourse on the subject of halal and particularly raise questions on how halal in practice is applied, evaluated or rendered in the corporate brand world. It may also ultimately define the relationship between the halal world and the corporate brand world and the extent to which they can accommodate each other. According to branding specialists and practitioners a brand is prominently about identity, image, culture and values among many other attributes. It is also emphasised that a brand's identity is multiple and dynamic. If we accept these formulations as given and then look at what halal is, we find that that halal has similar and/or identical attributes. Wherein lies the distinction then?

In one respect it can be argued they are literally worlds apart, occupying different symbolic universes: corporate branding is a modern marketing construct; halal is a first order religious principle in Islamic ethical tradition and law. They constitute vastly different categories of thought and practice. One is grounded at least in its contemporary form in the values of consumerism; the other in what is in many ways contrary religious conceptions about the moral order of society. In another respect, even the doctrine that found favour in Western Europe in the 19th century that religion and economic interests are separate and antithetical is no longer advanced with unquestioning assurance and has long since been abandoned as untenable. If in theory they were advanced as distinct, they were in fact always intertwined (Tawney 1954). Such stark dichotomy never found fertile ground in Islam. Whatever their basic differences are, the principles and rules of halal can be applied and in fact have been applied to the brand domain- however limited in scope. The fundamental requirement is that where a composite category is to be created the supremacy of halal is to be paramount. Only in this way can the corporate brand assume a real halal identity. While the *Sharia* (Muslim law) may not prohibit consumerist excesses in the context of what is halal or haram in Islam it may nonetheless view it as "Makrooh", meaning "hateful" or undesirable: the minimum that would be socially permissible. The interpretation of this concept is couched in terms of that which is morally reprehensible but legally permissible (Abd Al Ati 1977; Levy 1957). What this means is that: if brand is in one way or another an exemplar, a model, of consumerist society and its values, then the coupling of halal and brand will raise serious problems of credibility if not legitimacy sooner or later. For the brand to dissociate itself from abject consumerism and strive to gain credibility it must therefore first and foremost have a religious moral compass. This strategy will not by itself constitute sufficient conditions to secure legitimacy and credibility but it may satisfy key necessary conditions on the road to acceptance. Depending how genuine it is in terms of satisfying processes of evaluation and validation, then it would have a constituency with which it can align itself, among the varied interests contesting the merits of the project.

The Brunei Halal Brand: What it Offers, What it Signifies?

Other than the fact that the global halal brand is Brunei government owned and inspired commercial initiative, only very limited details are known which can shed light on various perspectives of the project. Among the things that we know is that the Brunei halal brand is not a brand that is conceived to sell products of its own making. Rather it is a corporate brand which brands or will brand other manufacturers products and offer them for sale to consumers. In other words it is purely and simply a brand name: one of a specific kind that does not make its products, provide ingredients for them, store, package or deliver them to the point of sale. If that is the case then it begs the question what does it offer the consumer other than its name? And therein lies its complexity and a considerable source of the potential problems it might face. The most outstanding is how is it going to control, monitor and evaluate all the various categories of products produced at so many different locations under its brand, if assumptions about its wide range of products are correct? Brunei has developed a relatively sound and detailed halal certification and audit regime and the brand corporation has also issued its own guidelines for use by product manufacturers' of the Brunei halal brand (See Ministry of Industry & Primary Resources 2007). At the outset however the potential for conflict of interest is obvious: with Brunei government directly or indirectly involved in or controlling both sides of the operation- albeit by different arms of the government. For the government to allow adequate or sufficient independence it would need to rely on a competent professional entity in the countries where participating companies are located for monitoring, supervision and certification. From these documents it also appears that the system relies too heavily on occasional audit, instead of regular and continuous, monitoring, supervision and certification in order to maintain the integrity and credibility of halal status of products from the point of production to the point of sale. Apart from certification, there is in fact no mention of the latter processes in the Brunei documents and it is unclear whether they will form part of the Brunei system. Nor is it clear how product certification will be controlled and applied on a regular basis. At least on this score existing halal systems in Australia appear more rigorous on paper than the Brunei's certification and audit regime.

The Brunei brand, however, makes one significant contribution: the very name by which the product is to be known, apprehended and identified universally. And it is on this name that the foundation of the project rests and which ultimately determines its future success. It will of necessity be a composite name that will at once wield halal into a brand complex. The name therefore will signify and embody multiple characteristics: one that validates products under its name upon presumably stringent procedures as authentic halal products that are free from haram contaminants. However important it is, the issue is not so much the name as its cultural signification, what its claims are and the extent to which such claims are credible in terms of halal norms and standards. Equally important is how the brand is packaged and presented for maximum effect in such a way that it can appeal to and capture the imagination of Muslim consumers worldwide. Claims about halal status, will first and foremost depend on how credible they are among halal stakeholders worldwide, particularly those that have the authority to influence public perceptions and ultimately validate halal practices. The Brunei objective to develop a corporate halal brand is in one important sense, by no means unusual as the corporate landscape is increasingly becoming a corporate brandscape. According to John Balmer (2006) "…corporate brands and their cultures and communities are stronger, wider and of greater consequence when compared to product brands and product brand cultures". There are many roads to branding and this is not only one of the most original but also one of the most challenging.

However the global halal brand as envisaged by Brunei is highly distinctive in at least two important ways: Firstly, as pointed out above, unlike major corporate brands, it does not manufacture its own products and would therefore presumably have lesser direct control over the production process than they do. That there are many manufacturers producing halal at widely dispersed locations is not by itself a major problem. The more likely challenge would be how to bring these under single unified control system. But, if dispersed manufacturing locations are accompanied by disparities in standards or lax methods of control, they can create problems for brand credibility. They can for example raise suspicions about halal integrity and engender perceptions that may adversely affect the reputation and image of branded products and the brand itself. By not being stringent and consistent in control, the brand makes itself open to allegations of non-compliance, or poor compliance with halal standards. In this scenario, Muslim stakeholders are unlikely to attribute failure to the system itself. Instead they are more likely to see it as a failure in which both the corporate brand and the certifier are complicit: the one for ignoring to follow prescribed standards; the other for failing to monitor and enforce them. It would not be inconceivable that they would be suspected of sweetheart deals to willfully circumvent the system and render it inoperative on the factory floor purely for financial gain. In the sense outlined above customer perceptions are extremely important for the brand. Once they take root, suspicions are difficult to undo. They form the stuff upon which rumour and innuendo thrive and take root as "fact". A brand would therefore do well to avoid anything that would remotely contribute to their formation.

Secondly the composite concept of a corporate halal brand brings into sharp focus two seemingly dissimilar categories representing a materialist conception on the one hand and a spiritual conception of society on the other. To what extent such an idea is going to succeed remains to be seen, but there is no doubt it is an attractive and ingenuous proposition from a global market perspective. Both of these issues are critical because they raise at different levels matters that are germane to the constitution, identity and image of the halal brand. There are many conditions that development of the nascent brand has to satisfy as well as potential challenges to overcome for it to be realised on the global landscape as worthy of the halal banner it carries. The halal identity on which its claims are largely based are critical as well as its strategies for engagement with those interests that may be opposed to or have concerns about a Brunei global halal brand. It appears however that the focus of Brunei has been more on the development of the commercial brand than on the halal perspective which is far more fundamental to the future success of the brand itself.

Problems of Specification of Products for the Brand

A new corporate global brand characterised as a halal brand such as the Brunei project is likely to be contested more broadly and at different levels than from the perspective of current evaluation and approval processes. While it is too early to say what products the Brunei halal brand will cover, it appears that starting with food and beverages it will cover the maximum range of products possible. What that means is uncertain at this stage of brand development. Its aim however is to capture as many products that are permitted to be halal approved as possible- a permission which is dependent on the *Sharia* and by extension the regulatory requirements of particular halal importing countries. Ultimately specification of the range of products will be necessary because each product category will have be tested and receive separate approval as halal.

At a recent halal conference in Melbourne (late 2007), Brunei and its brand project were given prominence not only by Brunei government Minister, but also by a senior representative of Elders Pty Ltd. and a representative of a major Melbourne Municipal Council which had signed a Memorandum of Understanding with Brunei. While there was no particular focus on specification of range of products nonetheless there was, at least, one speaker who made reference to the possibility of branding and/or certifying as halal tomatoes and other vegetable products. More striking was the exhibition of a few items just outside the conference hall, among them soccer balls and boots that bore halal inscriptions. At the very least these examples are highly contentious and their justification on the basis of the *Sharia* would be most tenuous. For this reason alone the introduction of products of questionable validity into halal branding, at a critical juncture has serious implications. Some Muslims would argue that offering such products as halal displays at worst willful ignorance and at best serious misrepresentation or basic misunderstanding of halal. In the first proposition if the speaker qualified his statement by saying that halal branding/certification in this instance would be necessary solely if it was widely known that the region from which the tomato came is contaminated by chemical residue or Nejis (filth) etc. then his proposition would have been justified. In the absence of that qualification tomatoes that are grown naturally and remain in a natural state (*Asl*), are not and can not be placed in a haram category and must be sold without the need for halal inscription or approval. There are many products that fall into that category and their approval as halal without justification such as that given above which points to a possible or real loss of halal status is not permissible in the *Sharia*. As a matter of principle everything is halal in Islam except for a very few products in the Quran and the Sunna that are specifically prohibited. This shows and is intended to show the expansive nature of that which is permitted (halal) as opposed to the very limited nature of things that are prohibited (haram) (See Ayan, 2001; Al Qardawi undated). To Muslims having a halal inscription on balls and boots would be utterly incredulous even if the possibility of making a case for it exists. In a scenario such as the one described above there is a real danger for a halal brand in that Muslims may perceive the above practices are insidious, designed to devalue the concept of halal and render halal products fetishistic in the extreme. It would confirm the view of those who may be inclined to believe that the whole branding enterprise is purely a marketing ploy devoid of any religious or moral or other social considerations.

Brand = Halal: Equivalence as a Strategic Tool

Brands can be versatile and innovative in their branding practices in that they can incorporate new concepts and products that are not integral to their tradition. A good example is the expansion of some major prominent food brands into the halal field. There is however a significant difference between halal-approved brand products and a global halal brand *per se* such as that which Brunei is creating. The former are unlikely to claim that their values and identity are based on Islamic tradition, as indeed they are not; whereas the latter would be able to assert its identity and values are based wholly on that tradition. In fact the reason d'être for the global halal brand is its Islamic cultural identity. It can not therefore exhibit, or incorporate cultural forms of identity that are antithetical to or dubious in Islam without serious risk to its very existence. This distinguishing characteristic not only asserts its Islamic identity, it also invites a crucial mental equivalence in marketing which is that the brand = halal, irrespective of any product in its brand profile, in a way no other corporate brand can. Brands such as Nestle or Unilever may and in fact do claim halal approval for a particular product batch/line produced at a given time by way of a halal inscription on their labels by an accredited authority, but they can not claim equivalence, nor can they claim cultural affinity or identity in the way the global halal brand can or is in fact bound to do in order to succeed. If the credentials of the global halal brand are well established, it will constitute an overwhelming advantage over other branded products producing halal on an irregular basis.

The claim to equivalence can however be misleading if taken too literally and without reservation. The primary distinction to be made is this: brand and branding pertain to an activity, a project or a milieu; halal to an instrument for control and management of that activity. However, it is possible to think of a particular brand as having so high a credibility rating that one can not think of it other than it being halal. This is the kind of equivalence that the brand should aim for overtime. Equivalence in this sense is a function of how Muslim customers worldwide would perceive and respond to the brand. If successful, it represents an unreserved confidence in and an unqualified endorsement of the halal status and identity of the brand.

Equivalence nevertheless is not the only optimal condition for halal brands all and sundry nor their sole objective. In this paper a halal corporate brand refers to a brand that trades globally as halal and whose product/service or full range of products/services are halal compliant and validated as such by a competent halal authority or certifying entity. Corporate brands outside this type can achieve by segmentation, that which the global halal brand can achieve by equivalence. (Furthermore, optimality of outcome does not readily lend itself to one-size-fits-all and can therefore, vary depending on the goals of the brand). What this means is that it is possible to segment a major brand into separate brand categories or sub-brands with one or more being exclusively halal. For example L'Oreal may choose to develop a new brand category under the banner of L'Oreal halal, with a profile of products catering for Muslim consumers in the first instance but ultimately with the objective of a broadly based all inclusive customer appeal and consumption. The same approach can be used by pharmaceutical products. What this shows is the flexibility, ease and ingenuity with which halal norms can be applied without compromising their integrity or the business activity or brand to which they are applied- with the proviso that the latter ought to comply with halal standards.

The Advantages of a Global Halal Brand

A global halal brand, if managed properly with integrity, would attract considerable goodwill and support from Muslims worldwide.

Importantly it can satisfy a huge unmet global demand and expand the quality and range of halal products readily available in global markets under an easily recognizable brand name, with which customers can identify. No other product or range of products would have a prospective customer base of the magnitude that a global brand can potentially have at its inception. This huge advantage offered by a ready-customer base should be sufficient cause to exercise great care in planning, development, management and implementation of the brand name corporation. That customer base is highly sensitive to issues of identity, image and authenticity of the branded products; they are therefore as likely to abandon the brand en masse as quickly as they had embraced it if these attributes are found to be wanting. Because a halal symbol has extraordinary customer attraction or pull, its power must therefore be nurtured and appreciated by the corporation embarking on the creation of a global halal brand. A global halal symbol would not be limited in its impact on the approximately 1.7 billion Muslim consumers worldwide; other non-Muslim consumers familiar with halal have shown they respond favourably or at least are not averse to purchasing halal products. Among its attributes are the following:

- It is a highly effective promotional tool for all products that carry the halal symbol
- Consumers identify strongly with the message it carries
- It imparts shared values and standards which are highly desired by consumers and are considered obligatory by most
- It conveys a moral code and ethical norms that consumers hold dear
- It engenders strong loyalty and attachment by consumers to products bearing the halal symbol
- It would give confidence to consumers worldwide that the products bearing the symbol are reliable and authentic halal products free from haram contamination

In recent times there has been a sharp increase in the number of products bearing halal inscriptions and logos on super market shelves which are imported mainly from Muslim- majority countries. The distinction between them and the global halal brand is that firstly they are not certainly global in their scope nor are many of them arguably brands at all- certainly not of the corporate type. Instead they are simply products with a halal inscription or logo, mainly in Arabic script utilising the high recognition value and popularity of halal to legitimatise their products to penetrate the market. On the face of it, some of the labels reveal that they are approved by a legitimate halal certifier, others by a self appointed halal certifier but many also appear unauthorised and carry no marks or stamps of an authorising entity. This reflects the serious deficiencies inherent in the current system of certification. One of the main issues this raises is whether the word halal particularly in its Arabic form is generic or whether it can be subject to rules governing trade marks if used by itself or as part of a composite symbol representing a brand. In all probability given its widespread use it can not be viewed as anything other than a generic term. Another issue is how to distinguish the global halal brand markedly from other competing symbols- even if they do not constitute brands- because the word halal is so central to the to the recognition, identity and image of all halal approved products. A global halal brand as a purely marketing tool is unlikely to enjoy universal acceptance among Muslims and may in fact expose it to serious criticism. Its Islamic imperative must therefore always be paramount in the way it is constituted, designed and presented.

Conceptualising "The Global" in the Halal Brand

A halal brand with a prominent national reference, such as a Brunei halal brand, faces the risk of limiting its scope and potential. It may for example restrict its acceptance, appeal and operational capabilities to a national sphere and beyond that make little or no traction at the international level. Given the potential shortcomings of a national reference point for the brand, it is imperative that the global perspective be brought sharply to the fore. This is not just a matter of nomenclature. Halal is universal and it is understood by Muslims worldwide to be universal. A global reference will help underpin that understanding. It ought to be therefore part of the brand in either of two ways or both:

- As an integral part of the name of the Brand and/or
- As the most outstanding feature of its promotional profile

However the key to the brand's development, operation and credibility is the halal standard. Not only does it form the basis for the claim of the brand as a global phenomenon but it is also the foundation upon which the halal brand is constructed, legitimised and given a religio-cultural identity. In this context the global halal standard constitutes a set of rules, processes and procedures that are alternatives to or otherwise supersede the many disparate individual country based regulations and procedural requirements. The rules and procedures in the proposed global halal standard(s) would not be new. Many of the provisions are already part of existing halal certification systems applied in fulfillment of individual country requirements. Because they are based on the *Sharia*, they have a high level of uniformity but with significant small variations. Most Muslims would subscribe to the view that since the halal standard(s) is a *Sharia* based universal standard(s), it should therefore be uniform throughout the world- hence the widespread recognition of the need for a global halal standard system. The formulation and presentation of the standard as global not only asserts the universality of the halal standard(s) as understood by Muslims but also underscores its *Sharia* foundations. The aim of this approach would be to entrench the role and image of the brand as a globalising, universalising halal agent. The characterisation of the standard(s) as global also reflects its consistent logical relationship with the global halal brand. By contrast if the brand were to rely on current national based standards their incongruity/mismatch would be manifest: a global brand operating under one among many national halal systems. That it is a global halal brand, not merely a halal brand or simply a Brunei specific brand, must also be made explicit, as pointed out above, in the naming of the brand or its presentation and marketing or both in order to expand its appeal. This approach has the potential to attract widespread support among Muslims who are convinced of the ethical supremacy of halal in commercial affairs. The linkage of the global brand and the global standard would also be an invaluable strategic and marketing tool that is likely to increases the confidence of consumers worldwide in the legitimacy and authenticity of the products under the brand.

Conclusions

There is no reason to suppose that Islam is antithetical to business or that the two occupy separate and coordinate domains. Throughout its history Islam has encouraged business enterprise. In this context the practice of branding and the use of brand as an aid to business promotion, as a corporate entity, as a symbolic representation of its culture or as a distinguishing mark of one business from another do not by themselves deviate from Muslim expectations of business practice. However Islam sets out ethical norms and standards to regulate commercial activity. These are based on the principles of halal and haram. Compliance with them is essential for brand legitimacy and credibility.

The image, credibility and success of the brand itself is largely dependent on structures and systems of evaluation, monitoring and control aimed at sanctioning and certifying the halal status of the brand and its products at any given time and place. Credibility is adversely affected to the extent that these systems are perceived by various interest groups and authorities who have a stake in the halalness of the products to be inadequate, deficient and/ or corrupt. If for example they do not meet or are simply perceived not to meet the standards prescribed in the *Sharia* or practices under which they are produced are contrary to or otherwise devalue these standards, the very legitimacy of the brand itself comes into question. In these circumstances it will not be able to sustain its credibility as a halal brand at all. What this underscores above all is the need for the brand to develop and rely on an underlying system of global rules, procedures and standards that are independent from but work in close cooperation with the branding organisation. These have to be given the widest possible publicity so that consumers come to accept the view that the production and practices of the brand are validated halal on the basis of the universal standard, and are therefore beyond reproach. The possibility however must always remain that this view may be contested by groups who may question its validity in one particular or another.

Apart from what products are being branded, there is equally the important question of how the underlying identity of a global halal brand is constructed and actualised. At one level, there is the issue of specificity of the brand i.e. what categories of products are being assigned for branding. At another level there is the issue of how the multiplicity of products can be consolidated in substance under one halal brand. As to the question of who is branding or whose brand is it, it is not a sufficient basis to proceed simply on the premise that it is a Brunei Government commercial initiative and therefore has Islamic origins. This may confer some degree of legitimacy on the project, but certainly not the critical impetus necessary for a global halal brand to succeed. That it is a Brunei project by itself potentially invites other Muslim governments with similar or even better halal credentials to contest it or compete with it. In fact Malaysia has had a series of discussions with Australia on a venture to establish Malaysia as a global "Halal Hub." The extent to which the two rival concepts may coexist in a competitive international framework or come into more serious conflict remains to be seen. Both projects are to a greater or lesser degree working on the expectation of Australian cooperation or support. Australia's support is particularly important for Brunei because it is the main, if not the only source of the products on which the whole brand enterprise rests. These are not, however, the only countries in South East Asia competing for a major share of the global halal market. Indonesia, Philippines, Singapore and Thailand are all developing projects aimed at capturing a slice of the global demand in halal products.

Chapter 6

Halal Development: Beyond the Rubber Stamp Syndrome

Introduction

Every once in a while as part of normal review and planning processes it is important to take stock of what a group, an organisation, or an entity does or has done in order to assess its performance: what it has accomplished and what it has failed to accomplish against set objectives. It gives these entities opportunities to renew their activities, expand their horizons, address their failures and shortcomings, reform themselves to meet new challenges, open up new opportunities and improve their existing performance. I point this out so that we can reflect on and take stock of where we are as a halal community: that is to say as a business community, as government authorities and as certifying bodies whose primary purpose it is to develop and facilitate halal trade and commerce. We have come a long way and we have a longer more arduous way to go.

The Halal Community and Trading Halal

The halal community expressed in this way is by no means limited to these groups I have just mentioned. The most important group in this community is the customer, the Muslim customer and also the global non-Muslim customer as well as those business enterprises that trade in halal goods and services or want to embrace halal and enter the worldwide halal market. There are also other stakeholders such as ulemas, academics and others that are knowledgeable about halal and haram and have a stake in its successes and failures. Halal is not an exclusive concept for Muslims only but an inclusive one for everyone. Those who want to be part of halal by producing it, consuming it or trading in it are free to do so. That is the beauty of halal and that is why it is universal. There are no unreasonable restrictions or discriminatory barriers to halal trade. Halal as a concept and in practice is conceived in Islam as facilitator par excellence of trade, except in a few specified products and services. The only requirement for manufacturers and producers is compliance with a set of halal standards. Once halal compliance standard(s) are met it opens up a huge market of approximately 1.7 billion Muslim potential consumers globally and perhaps a similar number of potential non-Muslim consumers who are willing or would not be averse to the consuming halal. For the Muslim community there is no nobler and greater reward in making halal a worldwide phenomenon than God's reward. Reference to the demographic population magnitude of the global Muslim community is important to underscore the material benefits as well as the spiritual rewards so that we can appreciate the potential scope of halal in the world and the responsibilities we have in developing it to its full potential. Are we ready and capable of meeting this challenge? I am not so sure and I will say shortly why.

Halal Authorities' Positive Contribution and the Deep Seated Problems that Remain

I am not in a position to comment on, nor am I qualified to evaluate the performance of governments and halal authorities in relation to halal specific activities. To be able to do so would require that I have appropriate knowledge, possess adequate information or evidence to support my arguments: evidence and knowledge which I admit I do not fully have. This however does not restrain me from making observations, expressing views and sentiments, making considered judgments and giving advice about matters which I think ought to be done in respect of improving halal trade and the institutions that deal with facilitating that trade. In particular there are good reasons to examine the serious problems I believe we face and to propose appropriate solutions that may overcome them. What I can say at the outset however is that the most important role and responsibility in halal affairs is that which is exercised by halal authorities in halal importing countries. They are the linchpin upon which all other halal institutions are dependent for their operation and existence. Whether they (the authorities) are an arm of government, or a corporatized entity (which appears to be an emerging trend), businesses would not have an international halal trade without them, Muslim consumers would not have the range and quality of halal products made available to them without them and halal certifying organisations and systems-of-control would not have existed or operated as effectively as they are without them. It is therefore important to give them due credit for their pioneering work in halal. It is appropriate that I take this opportunity on behalf of the halal community to applaud their work to-date, and to say at the same time that the work we all have to do is barely begun, and that greater challenges lie ahead to take halal to the next level of development: a level that is international in scale, vision and objectives. This orientation however requires different, more sophisticated instruments and higher professional standards than we had hitherto relied upon and utilised for our progress to-date.

Having commended the work of halal authorities, I am not confident that I can applaud our overall progress in halal and I am inclined to think that our progress and performance has a lot to be desired. If that is the case, then what are the key problems that we face and how are they hindering the development and progress of halal trade and commerce? These are the questions we have to ask of ourselves. But to pose these questions requires us above all to be honest with ourselves, to identify issues of concern and to be candid in the way we examine our performance and conduct, both at the professional level and in terms of our commitment and duty to Islam and by implication to halal trade and commerce. We must not blind ourselves to the facts. To do so would mean that our development will remain stunted and our potential and professional goals for halal will remain unrealised. I am sure none of us wants that to happen. If the various criticisms leveled at halal practices are valid, to a greater or lesser extent, it is not because of what halal stands for or represents but because of our failings as a halal community: the way we have rendered it and misrepresented it to the world at large and to business enterprises in particular.

The Universality of the Halal Standard and the Persistence of Parochial interests

So let's take stock. Many of the major problems of halal certification stem from our failure to sufficiently appreciate or apply basic halal rules, principles and values. As we ought to know in Islam halal and associated concepts comprise a universal ethic. The utilisation of halal is not for Muslims alone but for all mankind. This means that it is a universal standard or set of standards which ought to be in practice uniform or highly uniform throughout the world. What this clearly tells us is that Islam does not recognise a distinct or purely national halal standard- only a universal one. It can be argued however that this does not necessarily invalidate the existence of a national standard in so far as it is based on and is consistent with the universal *Sharia* standard. That is in fact true. But to say that there is a distinct Malaysian, Indonesian or Saudi halal standard gives the impression that they are somehow different or deviate from the universal halal standard. It suggests also that they have a separate, legitimate existence and value independent of the universal *Sharia* standard. This is not and cannot be the case. A halal standard that is different or deviates from the universal norm is not only factually wrong it also negates or otherwise diminishes the value of the concept and its practical uses. To assert the primacy of a national standard is to say by implication that there is either no universal halal standard or that even if there is one it is subsidiary or not efficacious. I am sure no one among us would in anyway uphold or subscribe to any of these propositions. To do so we would be contrary to Islamic thought and practice. It is not difficult to understand why the national model became the only model for halal certification. It is due largely to both historical and practical reasons. Halal exports are a relatively recent development. They require certification to meet national regulatory requirements of individual halal importing countries. Explanations such as this one may be valid, but they do not tell us why the universal standard has not been presented by halal importing counties as a single uniform standard for all Muslim countries.

It is obvious that over the years we have by our own actions relegated the universality of halal to a dubious, indeterminate and inaccessible background. The question then is why do we continue on this path? Why do we sustain national standards that are conflicting and confusing to enterprises and to consumers alike? And why can't we reassert the universality of halal and the uniformity of its standard(s). The most likely explanation is that the proliferation of the national standard has come about more likely by default than by deliberate or planned action. Part of the reason for the emergence of the national approach is that we have not simply developed the halal ethic into a uniform code of practice that business enterprises can easily adopt and comply with in producing halal goods and services. Equally importantly we have not thought through how to represent, facilitate and render halal in international markets. Furthermore the prevailing tendency to assert the paramountcy of national interest has contributed to a weakening of the universal principles in halal trade and commerce. But the fact remains that ascribing independent existence to a national standard is to misconceive and misrepresent halal. These factors in my view have given rise to a narrow particularism and contributed to the proliferation of national halal standards. And once this practice has taken hold and consolidated over the years we have lost sight of the fundamental tenet of the universality of the halal standard and the uniformity of its practices.

Reasserting Halal Norms and Standards

It is now long overdue to reverse this trend of halal misrepresentation and for halal authorities in Muslim countries to develop and agree on a uniform halal standard. I can hardly emphasise the value of this as a reform initiative. If we do this it will undoubtedly be our greatest accomplishment in the field of halal trade and commerce. The task at hand stands now as a pointed challenge to our commitment to one of the most fundamental principles of Islamic values- the principle of universality inherent in halal and haram. To emphasise the necessity of having a uniform halal standard or set of standards, however, does not mean that their provisions need to be the same in every particular. On the contrary they can accommodate national specific requirements in the form of added provisions. This can however be done only in the context of the uniform halal standard. In this way the universal rules, principles and values shall be reasserted as being paramount and national requirements relegated to being subsidiary additions derived from and/or based on the former. In this schema the reversal is necessary to clarify the relative value in the relationship between the two components if indeed the national particularist reference is justified or valid at all- which many Muslims would argue is not. A period of one year may be allocated to complete this task with possible time extensions if need be.

The Rubberstamp and its Negative Consequences for Halal Certification

It is now more than thirty years that halal has emerged as a noticeable, though vaguely recognisable and somewhat distinct component of international trade. Its emergence may herald a future in which it is widely accepted as a permanent term in the lexicon of that trade. The progress of halal certification however has been extremely slow. Potential non-Muslim halal consumers and producers barely understand it much less have sufficient confidence to utilise it as a standard to be complied with or as an underlying ethic in trade and commerce. There has not been any discernable or concerted effort to promote halal or to make it part of education and training. And yet halal is fundamental to understanding Islam and Islamic culture and values that underpin trade and commerce. Halal was prior to this period very limited in scope: limited that is, in the product categories it covered which in fact meant only meat; it was also limited in international product demand and in the resources and know-how it required to facilitate the trade. It required little or no specific knowledge or specialisation of any kind to validate or certify it and in most cases no credentials other than being a Muslim with basic understanding of how Muslims slaughter animals; and to know as every Muslim does that pigs and alcohol are haramrudimentary understanding that requires no education, no knowledge, no profession and no credentials whatsoever. One powerful tool for halal validation dominated the halal landscape: it was and continues to be the halal rubberstamp. So resilient and omnipresent is it as a halal validating tool that it dominates the halal landscape to this day. It has become the-be-all-and-end-all of halal certification. If the system demands other practices to be followed or prescribes standards to be met then they are superficially or minimally complied with or in most instances ignored altogether, by those organisations assigned to oversee its application-the halal certification societies. The reason is not that the people and organisations that do this are necessarily bad or malevolent; a more likely explanation is lack of competence and overall poor educational and professional profile of the practitioners of halal certification. Of course self interest is also a strong motivating force. Overwhelming reliance on rubberstamp certification assures its practitioners minimum input into provision of services and maximum financial returns.

The effect of this pattern of development on halal certifying organisations has been to breed a culture that values naked self interest above all else and devalues knowledge and professionalism which are the key components of excellence, growth and development of organisations and their systems of operation. Many existing halal certifiers seem blissfully unaware of the negative and debilitating impact of their poor performance on the halal system as a whole and how destructive it is for the credibility and image of halal trade or else are unconcerned. Even if they were fully aware, it is most likely that these organisations would have been incapable of reversing the deterioration in halal reputation because of the low level of their knowledge and professional competence. But the fact remains that they know no better than that which they do and to which they have grown accustomed. A curious and pervasive self confidence has taken hold of an untenable, but nonetheless self-perpetuating system that is devoid of any positive attributes to commend it. In any other organisational environment, outside the Muslim sphere, the damage these societies and the model they represent are causing to the idea and application of halal would have been utterly obvious. In any other professional organisational setting they would have met at the very least with disapprobation and subjected to serious scrutiny which in all likelihood would have threatened their survival. As it is that they operate in a Muslim sphere unfortunately shields them from such scrutiny which in turn ensures their continued existence. There is good reason to suppose and a widespread view among Australian Muslims that some of these organisations are being protected and that their survival as halal certifying entities is not due to anything other than that people with sufficient power have a personal interest in them and ensuring their preservation. This is an assumption which carries considerable weight in the absence of credible alternative explanations for their continued existence. Without such support from authorities they would have collapsed under the weight of their malpractices and incompetence. The audit report in this book refers to a business that was and may still be producing halal and haram in the same premises but contrary to *Sharia* rules was granted approval and supervised over many years by an accredited halal certifier. The same certifier is reported in the media to have recently granted halal certification to a Hungry Jacks franchise presumably without the knowledge of that company. It prompted the chief Executive to disclaim that *Hungry Jacks* products had ever been or claimed to be halal. He is reported to have said, "Hungry Jack's can confirm halal certified items are not now, and have never been available from any Hungry Jacks restaurant…" (*Hume Leader* 7 February 2012 see article appendix 3). If this true, it defies credibility how an Islamic society could act in blatant contravention of basic Islamic rules by granting halal certification to a manifestly haram establishment. More incomprehensible is that this society has not been asked, to our knowledge, by the relevant authorities to show cause why it acted in the way that it did.

Lack of Proper Criteria and Professional Competence

There is considerable weight of information to support the above claims. So prevalent is the occurrence of these practices that they constitute the norm rather the exception. They point to deep underlying problems in the way halal certifying organisations are accredited and how their accreditation is renewed. A few examples will suffice. The guidelines of overseas halal authorities are understood to place considerable importance on professionalism, accountability and transparency as primary conditions for accrediting halal certifiers. They also insist that certifiers incorporate into their structure Muslim scholars and scientists in an advisory capacity. The criteria may look good on paper, however, their practicality and relevance are highly questionable given the certifiers' incomes and capacities. Irrespective of their income, the majority of organisations are so small that they can not accommodate this into their structure. But they all claim that or rather maintain the fiction that they have incorporated these committees into their structure when if fact they have not done so and in all probability can not. A cursory examination of the list they present to halal authorities would show a preponderance of ordinary Muslims who do not have any particular knowledge of halal or science. In other words the list in as much as it refers to persons having particular credentials and competence is purely fictitious. One can only speculate that the list satisfies these criteria only in the realm of the imaginary, which seems acceptable to authorities! The authorities know too well that these criteria for accreditation are not working now nor have they worked in the past. If that is the case, then one might well pose the question: what is the point in establishing guidelines and criteria for halal certifiers when it is patently obvious that they are impractical and can not be fulfilled for other reasons as well. As a halal community, we have declared and insisted upon criteria for accreditation that are not genuine; that can not in anyway be applied in practice and which can reasonably lead people to think that there may be hidden ones that are being applied instead or that none are being applied at all. It raises the legitimate question how transparent and accountable the system is and more seriously how credible the whole halal system is!

There are other examples that are equally if not more perplexing. It should be reasonable to expect from any organisation with an average competence and particularly one with a service provision and communication as a large component of its work to have a good educational and professional profile. The reality on the ground is starkly different. Many of the Muslim personnel in leadership positions or at the coalface of relationship with business corporations have not completed formal schooling or may not be sufficiently literate or competent enough to carry out the tasks they are required to perform. Except for a very few those that have good credentials generally fare little or no better in performance or contribution to halal than those who don't. In fact there is no demonstrable commitment to halal development that distinguishes qualitatively those with seemingly appropriate credentials from their less credentialed counterparts. Be that it may competence and educational profile of organisations and individual personnel are conspicuously absent as criteria from the guidelines of any of the halal authorities in accrediting halal certification organisations. If education and professional competence are not valued as key conditions to obtain accreditation, then it would follow that there should be no expectation of good performance from halal certification organisations. But there are wider ramifications: the image of halal may forever be damaged and with it any confidence corporations and consumers have in the halal system. The failure of authorities to address these problems over a long period of time have made them more acute than they would otherwise be, and the need for solutions ever more pressing. And the simple issue that confronts us all is this: is there a collective will to do something about these multilayered problems that have been ignored and have consequently accumulated over the years or is there not? What is needed above all is a comprehensive, not a piecemeal or a superficial reform- but one that at least entertains the possibility that a significant proportion of existing halal certification organisations will be replaced with far more competent organisations that are better able to represent halal values, norms and standards.

The Multilayered Deficiencies of the "Islamic Society" Model of Halal Certification

All past and present halal certification organisations are built on a particular organisational model, which is that of an "Islamic society" or rather, the conception of an Islamic society which is prevalent in many Islamic environments in western countries. The reason why this is important is that most halal authorities grant accreditation only to entities that are designated "Islamic societies". In particular they exclude in theory and practice individually owned or proprietary companies from being accredited to certify halal food. But the undeniable truth is that the overwhelming majority are entities that are either directly or indirectly privately owned by individuals or groups of individuals. The problem is not so much that they are so owned but the fiction that they are exclusively Islamic societies when in reality they are not. What is obvious is the stark disconnect between that which the halal authorities say is the model and criteria for accreditation of certifiers and the reality on the ground which is that most claim to be Islamic societies when there is no indication they are what they say they are. If halal authorities conscientiously applied their own guidelines and criteria for halal certifiers, the majority would lose their accreditation on the basis of this criterion alone.

There are many other problems associated with the conception of Islamic society as a model or criteria for certification of halal food. The presumption upon which this conception is based is a flawed one. It is premised upon the supposition that Islamic societies are *per se* competent, properly constituted, broadly based Islamic community organisations with ownership, composition and management vested in that community. For the overwhelming majority this has not certainly been the case. In fact none of these characteristics are true of most halal certification organisations that claim to be Islamic societies. In every respect you look at them, there is no more graphic illustration of a disconnect between what Islamic societies claim to be and appear to be on the one hand and what they in fact are on the other. Islamic societies are often the predominant form of Islamic organisations in most western countries. The most common and widespread are mosque based Islamic societies. Other types are relatively very few and they include some whose hold on the term is very tenuous. The majority of halal certifiers are not mosque societies or mosque based societies even though some are made to look as if they are. However it is not uncommon they have the term Islamic society or the term halal as part of their name. The assertion of and attachment to the name by halal certifiers is understandable. It is this: halal authorities insist that an entity be an Islamic society as a condition for granting accreditation as a halal certifier. To satisfy this condition they claim that which they are not. If they don't they may well lose their accreditation to certify halal.

In Australia "Islamic societies" as part of their historical development are identified with and are in many cases controlled by individuals from the same country, town or village. A significant proportion express their nationality in their name i.e. Croatian Islamic Society, Turkish Islamic Society etc. They have no broad based Islamic focus or identity. Very few have a broad nationality mix. Consistent with this pattern a halal certification entity calling itself an Islamic society, is often controlled by individuals or groups that have narrow ethnic affiliation base and/or close common interest. Membership of the organisation which is often closed to outsiders is similarly drawn from the same stock based of national, ethnic or village affiliations. As a result what emerges is a pattern of unchanged membership or executive in Islamic societies that have been in existence for over many years, except where death, conflict or other unfortunate circumstances intervene and force unavoidable and unpredictable change. An important feature of Islamic societies is that their structures for representation of a broader Muslim community or even a single national community is weak and in some cases non existent. Annual General Meetings, an indispensible part of organisational imperatives, are seldom held and if held at all are contrived affairs solely designed to satisfy the provisions of the Act under which they are registered. There are a number of organisations that have not held such meetings for many years. The result is pervasive poor management, accountability and operational practices which render them incapable of introspection, review and reform.

The above organisational issues raise the question whether the Islamic society model is the appropriate model for halal certifying organisations and whether it should be conditional on granting halal accreditation. On the face of it there are no positive qualities that commend it as a model to be emulated. On the contrary it is a clear example of the kind of organisational model that should be avoided. If that is the case then, making this model a key criterion for accrediting halal certifiers sends the wrong signal which is that authorities are satisfied with and are supportive of the model and its practices. It is now time for halal authorities to reconsider their position. If the model has proved anything in the past thirty five to forty years it is that it is not a suitable model for halal certification organisations or for any other organisation for that matter. At the very least they should send a strong signal that the model in the light of its multilayered deficiencies shall be re-evaluated and that the practices that had hitherto been tolerated will come under serious scrutiny. On the basis of the above considerations it is true to say as a general proposition that the halal system is as good as the halal certifying societies that operate it. In other words the system merely reflects both the strengths and weakness of these societies. In practical terms we should not expect the system to produce good results when the foundations on which it is built are extremely weak.

Confusion over Basics in Halal and Haram: An Example

The organisational culture which prevails in the "Islamic society" model is one which validates unconscionable practices that are clearly against the very rules Islamic societies are required to uphold. The conflicting and arbitrary nature of decision making of this model adds to the confusion which characterises the conduct and performance of these societies. To illustrate this point a halal authority has denied approval to a business establishment producing halal meat on the grounds that its premises was next to another which was producing pork and furthermore deregistered the halal certifier under which it had operated. In another case the same authority approved as halal-registered a company that produced halal meat and pork under the same roof in the same premises but unlike the other certifier which was deregistered, its accreditation remained in force and unaffected. This clearly the reverse of what should have happened according to the rules but in this instance it was not clearly the case. I chose this example because it can not in any way be justified in the context of halal rules and standards; it highlights what is wrong with the system as a whole. There are no rational grounds why such conduct is sanctioned as meeting halal standards. Other than the fact that it is contrary to halal rules, it brings to the fore sharp inconsistencies in the application of *Sharia* rules. In such circumstances it would be reasonable to expect business enterprises to wonder what the rules actually are. If the ethical underpinnings are removed or their validity in practice ignored, then it is no halal system at all!

Many so called "Islamic societies" have been in the business of certification for many years. Whether they are privately owned under the guise of "Islamic society" as most of them are or Mosque based entities, the fact remains that they are both operated as privately owned entities and their benefits are mainly derived by an individual, a family or a closely knit group rather the a broadly based Muslim community. The Islamic reference is intended to hide this fact. So, if they are neither real Islamic societies nor representatives of a broad based Muslim community then it stands to reason that the criterion be removed as a condition for granting accreditation and better alternative set of criteria be considered. A typical halal certification society is a very small organisation with very few personnel, often no more than two or three. Those with four or five are the exception. The difference in numbers merely reflects group dynamics in that incorporated in the personnel are those members who have a financial interest in it. The export businesses with which halal societies deal with and provide services to are organisations with complex needs. The kind of societies we have as certification bodies are not well equipped and do not have the capacity or credentials to provide the sophisticated services that global business organisations need. All too often they fail to satisfy the basic conditions of their accreditation for example appropriate monitoring and supervision. Lack of capacity makes regular supervision visits highly improbable which leaves companies do as they will through no fault of their own.

Creating a New Professional Model of Halal Certification Organisations

Given the unsuitability of the "the Islamic Society" model and its many operational deficiencies it would be appropriate if not necessary that a radically different model be adopted. Such a model would have clear and unambiguous Islamic foundations based on the *Sharia* in respect of its halal and haram operations without being necessarily an Islamic society. Consistent with this underpinning it would be a highly competent and professional model that can cater for the sophisticated needs of the modern age and complex modern enterprises. Unlike the current model it would be a model above all whose integrity and identity is not ambivalent and whose practices are not conflicted and problematic as the current one is but one whose path, direction and purpose is clear and unambiguous. Not only should it have a very good and sound understanding of halal and haram, it must at the same time be able to demonstrate that it can contribute to the development of halal trade and commerce. This does not mean simply certifying food, from which a certifier derives income, but active engagement in and contribution to the universal application of halal principles, norms and standards. Education and professional competence will be highly valued in this model so much so that those that do not meet these criteria would not be encouraged to apply nor be considered for accreditation if they do. The table below juxtaposes the contrasting characteristics of the current "Islamic society" model which may be considered for replacement and the recommended alternative professional model it may be replaced with.

Table 4 Comparative Models: contrasting characteristics

Current "Islamic Society" Model	Proposed Alternative Islamic Model
1. Islamic Society model with obscure identity.	Composite Islamic & professional model
2. Static model: lacks understanding of good management practices and good quality service provision; unresponsive to desired changes for improvement	Dynamic model: attuned to best practice in halal management and service provision and responsive to desired changes for improvement
3. Contribution (a): demonstrates no capacity or capability to contribute to the development or universal adoption of halal norms and standards	Contribution: contributes to the promotion, development, facilitation and application of universal of halal norms & standards

4. Professional competence: weak application of halal rules & rudimentary understanding of halal principles, compliance requirements and halal needs of business	Professional competence: has good educational profile, skills and know how on halal rules, principles, compliance requirements
5. *Sharia* injunctions & national regulations: applied, arbitrarily, crudely, inconsistently or not all	*Sharia* injunctions and national regulations: applied consistently, stringently with integrity & sensitivity
6. Ownership: closed & ambiguous based on individual, group or ethnicity; in rare cases on society	Ownership: open, individual, group or society based on clear identity and capability: criteria based
7. Identity: ambiguous, questionable, internally conflictual externally misleading; closed membership	Identity: clear and unambiguous with internal consistency and external clarity
8. Delivery of service: unreliable, generalised unspecific and unprofessional	Delivery of service: well defined, reliable, competent professional support services
9. Communication: distant, erratic and lacking clarity of direction & purpose	Communication: close, regular, appropriate and purposeful communication
10. Feedback on issues of concern: Unhelpful, irrelevant, inappropriate or misleading	Feedback: to the point, helpful and relevant to issues of concern
11. Audit: unfamiliar with audit principles, uses checklist designed, developed and controlled by non Muslims, pretentious, lacks substance and focus	Audit: targeted & focused; conceived, applied and developed for application and control by Muslims, good grasp of audit values and principles, improvement oriented

12. Certification: overwhelming use of rubber stamp as primary instrument of halal management and control	Certification: comprehensive use of halal principles, norms and standards with rubber stamp dependent symbol and validating instrument for halal processes
13. Contribution (b): makes little or no contribution to Muslim community development	Contribution: demonstrates adequate and tangible contribution to Muslim community development, commensurate with its resource capabilities
14. Reporting and record keeping: rarely reports its activities or does so only when instructed by authorities with also poor record keeping practices	Reporting & record keeping: reports at least annually to national and halal authorities as a matter of course and other times as need be with good record keeping practices

The Problematic Development of Halal Certification and the Entrenchment of the Rubber Stamp

Halal certifying organisations and their application of the halal standard had an uneven and problematic development over the years, often hidden from public view. Marked by vagueness and uncertainty in identity and conception as well as in purpose and direction, they stumbled into a business export scene with which they were totally unfamiliar and for which they were utterly unprepared and ill-equipped for the tasks they were to perform. These were further compounded by internal structural and operational weaknesses. Just as halal was about to enter the international stage in the 1980s, serious problems emerged in the red meat Industry in Australia (including halal Meat) which became the subject of a Royal Commission in 1982. The Royal Commission exposed grave malpractices in the certification of halal meat including lack of professionalism poor service provision and of corrupt practices. In the 90s certain corrective actions were taken by halal authorities regarding halal certification. But these changes were by no means extensive and were less a consequence of the findings of the Royal Commission than the product of internal conflict between a major certifier and a major halal authority. In the aftermath of these events which spanned five years new accredited organisations entered the halal certification scene. In these circumstances a measure of progress was made and as a consequence knowledge about halal increased considerably, albeit starting from a low base. This is the period when the conference circuit became common and networking among the halal community developed. In Australia, in only four years in the mid to late 1990s, a colleague and I held three International halal conferences which were attended by most certifiers and halal authorities. By comparison, since 2000 no international halal conference was held in Australia. This is due primarily to lack of competence by most halal certifiers to develop and promote halal trade and commerce. Not only has demand for halal risen sharply during this brief period of progress, but major corporations entered the halal export field in a big way. Whereas in the past halal clients were small companies with no greater demand for services than a certificate and a rubber stamp, in the 90's bigger and complex corporations with more sophisticated, multidimensional demand became a prominent feature of the halal landscape. Significantly while demand for halal know-how and sophisticated halal services is rising considerably, only a few of the halal certifiers are now capable of responding to these demands at the level of sophistication and knowledge required by corporations. There is a compelling need for greater professionalism in the provision of halal services. I urge you to look around at our resources, capabilities and competence and judge for yourselves whether we are up to the task. There is a clear indication that, with our current halal structures, we are not.

The view that certification with a rubberstamp is all that is needed for halal is well entrenched. And certification in this way has become a common practice among certifiers but with few exceptions. The thinking that still prevails is that halal is simple and rudimentary; all that a certifier needs is a stamp and certificate and a rudimentary know-how such as that I referred to- pigs and alcohol are haram stuff. I want you to reflect on the reality and the symbol of the stamp as the key and for some certifiers the only instrument for approving and validating halal. It is a striking and highly visible tool for the wrong reasons. It exemplifies what is wrong with the way we do things: a symbol of rubberstamp is not one that is based on knowledge, on progress, on inspection, on professionalism on satisfying demands of a modern age. On the contrary, it is a symbol that demeans and devalues halal and with it halal certification. It is based on fees for little unprofessional services to business. It shows in the most graphic way that the practitioners of rubberstamp certification are backward and unenlightened. It harms our reputation in the eyes of business enterprises that are engaged in or want to engage in halal and expect to receive professional services second to none. What I have just described to you as a mentality can in a sense be described as a rubberstamp syndrome. It can be defined as a symptom of a malaise, disorder or abnormal conditions in the halal system. What can we, or rather what should we do to remedy this situation?

Taking Stock and the Need for Reform

As shown in this essay, the case for change is a compelling one. The scope of our review of halal certification, if we have to have one, must be broad. It would be inappropriate to single out for criticism certain categories of organisations and not to look at the role of others in addressing our shortcomings and failures. To do so would be neither fair nor objective. There is also perhaps a better alternative. It is to forgo the review process particularly any investigative component in recognition of the fact that the problems we face are well known as set out in this paper. And while there may be a case for investigation to bring them to light it may be counterproductive to fully expose them at least on the grounds that it may serve no useful purpose to wash our dirty linen in the open. In this context it is sufficient to agree on a model to adopt and to discard the existing model(s) lock stock and barrel. This argument has considerable merit both for the reasons stated above and for the fact that it is far more expeditious than the alternative. Equally importantly it enables us to avoid any bitter recriminations that might ensue as a consequence of a heavily investigative review.

It would be wrong to suggest that there had been no attempts to bring about a measure of reform. In fact there was an ambitious one in which I was involved in and to which I have contributed. It was the formation of the World Halal food Council (WHFC) for which I wrote the guiding principles, objectives and constitutional provisions under the auspices of one of the halal certifiers in Australia. It was established in 2001 as an umbrella organisation for halal authorities and halal certifiers. It was formed with high hopes and great expectations as a forum to carry us forward and usher a new era of enlightenment, progress and professionalism at a global scale. Its objectives reflected these hopes and expectations and still do. It was to bring us together and give us a sense of purpose and direction, engender professionalism and best-practice in service provision to business enterprises, develop uniform standards, integrate our systems of control, represent us in international food, hygiene and food standards forums, equip us with the tools to achieve excellence in performance. The reality is most unfortunately that none of these hopes and expectations were even remotely realised. The fact is that it (the WHFC) has many internal and external problems. Internally it is largely inactive, uncoordinated and ineffective. It is not integrated internally as an entity nor integrated externally in any meaningful way with halal authorities. Above all it lacks identity, recognition and authority. The only authority it could possibly have is that which national authorities can invest in it. And it is nowhere apparent that that such concession to invest it with authority is forthcoming from anywhere now or in the future. It is our collective failure that the World Halal Food Council is weak and ineffective. My guess is that poor relations between halal authorities and among halal certifiers are hindering its progress. We can question whether we actually need WHFC. But even if we do not want to retain it in its current form, the concept it embodies is extremely valuable in that we need an umbrella organisation that unites us globally. It may be the WHFC, or the Muslim World League or any other. We must consider seriously the formation of such an entity. Without it the progress of halal as a universal phenomenon will be wanting.

Conclusion

Nothing is more damaging to halal development than the current state of obscurantism and paralysis of halal certification structures. It is imperative to act with determination on reform and have a clear vision of where we are going. There are five areas that need urgent action in order to develop a sound, efficient and effective halal control and management system. They are:

1. Developing a uniform halal standard
2. Adopting a suitable professional model for halal certification with attendant criteria for accreditation
3. Integrating halal development, as a key component, into the halal certification system
4. Establishing an umbrella organisation to oversee halal management and control (regional or global, preferably the latter)
5. Establishing an organisation to oversee and audit halal certifiers in major countries that produce or export halal food

None of these objectives are extremely difficult to achieve. In regard to the first, the existence of various national halal standards makes the task easier than it would otherwise be, particularly in view of the fact that all the national standards currently in operation are *Sharia* based standards. The various national standards therefore do not mean any substantive differences. Far from developing a brand new standard we shall be in fact, for the most part, integrating various national standards into a single universal standard. In substance, content and purpose they are all strikingly similar or more likely the same in many respects. The question therefore is not what has to be combined or integrated but only how they are to be combined and presented. This task as with other tasks of which it is part requires formation of a committee with the necessary credentials to perform it. Adopting a new model for halal certification organisations is sufficiently detailed in this paper and requires applicants to satisfy strict criteria based on professional competence and other standards common to professional organisations. Halal development is complex notion which combines these and other objectives including incremental improvement in halal certification, halal marketing, research, education and training. The fourth objective of an umbrella organisation for halal trade and commerce is central to the notion of halal development. Halal itself is a universal concept and requires a universal structure to match and represent its conceptual underpinnings. A suitable starting point for this kind of office would be the GCC countries, comprising Saudi Arabia, the United Arab Emirates, Kuwait, Qatar, Bahrain and Oman which has more common trade rules and structures than other comparable regions. Alternatively there can be two offices one in Asia and the other in the Middle East. Regarding the fifth objective an oversight organisation would play a critical role in enhancing accountability of halal certifiers and ensuring that they meet significantly higher performance standards than they currently do.

Chapter 7

A Halal Inspection Report of PPP Pty Ltd.*

Inspection Dates: 20-22 April 2009

Inspection conducted for: ABC Society

Consultant Inspector's Name: Abdul Ayan,

Establishment No: 1234

Name of Establishment being inspected: PPP Pty Ltd.

Establishment Type: Boning Room

Address: ————————————

Species processed in Plant: Lamb/ Mutton, Beef, Pork

Terminological Distinctions: Halal, non-Halal and Haram: In this document halal refers to food that is legally permitted by the *Sharia* (Muslim law) for consumption by Muslims and haram that which is prohibited; non-halal refers to food that is halal in origin (e.g. species) but is not killed, processed or validated in accordance with Muslim rules.

Purpose:

1. To assess and report on the adequacy of and compliance by the above establishment with halal production standards and processes
2. To validate the halal practices of the plant and the transfer of provision of halal certification services from DEF Islamic society to the ABC society.

N.B:

- The 'previous' halal certifier of the establishment is DEF Islamic Society
- The "incoming" certifier is ABC Islamic Society
- This report includes shaded synopses

The names of the organisations in this report have been changed to protect their identity except AQIS.

Introduction:

I was requested by ABC Islamic society to inspect PPP halal establishment and to report on its halal operations. Prior to the inspection I was not given any information about its operations other than that it is a halal registered meat producing establishment. I was also given to understand that on the instigation of the establishment an agreement had been reached for ABC society to replace the previous certifier- DEF society- and henceforth provide certification services to PPP. On the basis of the information I had I could make three reasonable assumptions:

A Halal Inspection Report of PPP Pty Ltd.*

1. That the services of the previous certifier had been terminated or are about to be terminated,
2. That the credentials of the plant as a halal establishment is not in question- even if improvements need to be made and,
3. That the primary purpose is simply to confirm and validate and report on the overall operations of the plant.

On all counts the reasonable assumptions that I made proved to be wrong as this report shows.

The Visit and Certification Issues

I visited PPP to inspect halal meat processing on the above dates. I saw no certificate that displayed, prominently or otherwise, the status of the premises as a halal registered establishment, as is generally required. Contrary to my earlier understanding it was unclear whether the establishment has transferred its supervision and certification services to ABC. I have not been presented with documents that show an in-principle agreement had been reached or that a transfer from one to the other has taken place, even though my visit was premised on the understanding that supervision henceforth shall be under the ABC society. What is puzzling is that despite my presence, the DEF society's supervisor was also present in the premises in that capacity. When I indirectly pointed out the duality of roles and the inherent conflict involved, I was told not to worry about it. This did not allay my concerns as the establishment was still using DEF certification documents and logo. It seemed to me that the establishment wanted to have one foot in each camp and particularly not to sever its relations completely with the DEF society. It was clear to me that this situation was untenable. I had with me certificates to cover the establishment's operations until the arrangement with the ABC society is formalised after the completion of inspection. It was becoming increasingly obvious that the establishment was neither ready nor sincere in wanting to transfer provision of certification services from the previous certifier to ABC society. This situation must not be allowed to continue and shall in any event resolve itself soon.

- There appears to be a confusion, indecision or disingenuity on the part of this establishment about which society it wants to certify and supervise its halal operations.

- The establishment has asked ABC to replace DEF as its certifier, but is still using DEF for supervision, certification and validation of its products as halal

- This position is untenable and ought to resolve itself within a month or so.

Parameters of Inspection Tasks

At the outset I saw my role in the following terms:

1. to assist the establishment to attain the prescribed halal standard(s)
2. to validate the halal system operating in the establishment once it has attained the above standard
3. to monitor and supervise the production and processing activities of the establishment to ensure the maintenance of and compliance with that standard.
4. to assess the establishment's halal production activities, to report to ABC on the level of its halal compliance and if necessary recommend an appropriate course of action

Reporting Method

This report is based on information, views and understandings based on or derived from the following sources:

(a) My knowledge and understanding of halal and haram principles and their application to food products

A Halal Inspection Report of PPP Pty Ltd.*

(b) My own observations during three inspection visits (on 20, 21 and 22 April 2009) to the establishment and the views I have formed during these visits
(c) Discussions with the Quality Assurance Manager at the establishment representing the business enterprise
(d) Discussions with AQIS inspector at the establishment representing the government
(e) Discussions with DEF society halal inspector representing the "outgoing" halal certifier
(f) Examination of the halal program presumably approved by DEF society, under which the establishment operates

Limitations of the Report

This is not a comprehensive report. It relies heavily on matters that could be easily observed, information that was made available or was readily available as well as on discussions with the personnel who were responsible for halal operations of the establishment. The report does not address some important issues such as washing procedures, movement and removal of waste material, bones and fat as well as the record of corrective actions that may have been taken by the plant from time to time. I did not seek this information nor was it made readily available to me.

Halal Program

I had a quick examination of the halal program. The establishment produces lamb/mutton, beef and pork in the same premises. It is clear that the program is inadequate, outdated and misleading. It has also other glaring deficiencies. This may be due to many reasons, most importantly lack of understanding or disregard of the fundamentals of halal production standards or both. It can also be due to the lack of proper guidance from the certifying society, namely DEF.

The program states that the main purpose of the establishment is to comply with the Indonesian halal standard and product specification.

That appears not to be the case. Irrespective of the contents of its program the establishment does not meet now nor could it have met in the past the Indonesian halal standard- or any Muslim country's standard. The production of pork in the premises makes this patently obvious. It is difficult to comprehend and even harder to justify how the establishment could have maintained its halal registration under these circumstances over the years. An unsatisfactory explanation may be that the program has not been reviewed since it was formulated in January 2007, as indeed it should have been. This does not detract from the fact that the establishment had been allowed to operate under a misleading and wholly unsatisfactory program that can hardly be said to have met export halal standards. The following observations underscore these conclusions.

The halal program also states that "Halal meat will be produced to the Australian standard". The claim that halal meat is produced to an unspecified Australian standard alone is novel and peculiar if not also misleading. Those who formulate halal programs should be careful to ascribe halal standards as emanating wholly from or having their source in non-Muslim entities. Halal standards are prescribed by Muslim authorities in overseas countries to which Australia exports halal products. They are based on fundamental principles of the *Sharia* (Muslim Law) and interpretations thereof, not on rules and values that are in any way independent of or inconsistent with the *Sharia*. Nevertheless it is possible to ascribe a halal standard to a certifying body only to the extent that the functions it performs and authority it exercises are derived from a competent halal authority in overseas halal importing countries under whose auspices the certifying body is registered.

The program content must adequately represent the factory's halal operations and practices. It does not satisfactorily do that. For example it asserts that "Meat and meat products destined for Indonesia will occur as the first run of the day when halal product is produced". The assertion is both outdated and misleading and does not reflect how the factory operates (see paragraph 2.8). The company, according to its Quality Assurance Officer, had exported to Indonesia but no longer does so. The fact however remains that it can not meet the Indonesian standard now, nor could it have done so in the past. The assertion that Indonesia is an export destination is yet again made on page one, of the "Inspector

A Halal Inspection Report of PPP Pty Ltd.*

System: Establishment Report As At: 2009-4-21", - a form that I am uncertain whether it is generated by factory management or by the AQIS Inspector. Importantly also it is not true to say that the halal production run occurs as the first run of the day. The same program contradicts it by saying that it will be done differently if halal can not take place on the first run of the day (6.1.3 (6)). There is a wide discrepancy between program claims and actual practice and a marked disconnect between both and halal requirements.

The understanding I gained from various people whom I have consulted is that timing of production-run is dictated mainly by management and production demands than by halal considerations. In other words a halal run is not always the first run of the day. In practice the establishment operates under the most minimum halal standards. Most ordinary Muslims, let alone Muslim authorities, would not validate the halal program as it currently is and many of the prevailing practices in this establishment would not be endorsed as being halal compliant. In the current environment in which the factory operates, absolute separation of halal and haram products is extremely difficult to maintain and haram (pork) contamination of halal is easy to occur.

- The halal program does not adequately represent the halal operations in the factory floor as it should. It is also outdated.

- In its current form it does not satisfy the Indonesian halal standards nor can it satisfy a broadly based halal standard.

- Contrary to the claim in the program, a halal production run is not always the first run of the day- the-claim is contradicted in the same program

Rails and Hooks

The program is, except for a passing and superficial reference, silent on the rails and hooks at product receival area in respect of halal. There is no reference in the program on how to prevent halal contamination that may result from hooks and rails being used for both halal and haram products (carcasses). Is a washing procedure applied to both and are separate hooks used for different categories of carcasses? (The program is also similarly silent on conveyor belts). There is one rail at the unloading entry point for halal, non-halal and haram, and the same hooks are used for all categories. This is highly problematic and unlikely to meet a genuine halal standard. There should at least be two rails with sufficient spatial separation as basic minimum requirements only where halal and non-halal are concerned. Nowhere does the program also address residue that may be left on the rails or the possibility of mix-up of hooks used for halal and non-halal or haram. Halal contamination is likely to occur more frequently in this than in most other areas, so clear and unambiguous operational procedures are necessary for it not to occur. The practices of the establishment in this section do not in any way comply with halal standard(s); in fact they sharply contravene them.

- Using one rail at entry point for halal and haram is problematic and does not conform to halal standard; the haram residue that may be left on rails would contaminate halal products.

- The potential for mix-up of hooks and their likelihood to carry haram residue is very high

- The practices in this section are not halal compliant; they utterly contravene halal standards.

Carton Marshalling/Holding Area

The carton marshalling area lies at the centre of the ground floor of the establishment. Along one side (east?) are the receival, classification and production/processing areas; along the opposite side are the freezer, chiller and blasting areas. On one side of the marshalling area a conveyor belt moves cartons from the non-halal/ haram section to be unloaded in this area. At the other end another conveyor belt moves cartoned halal products and both halal and haram converge into one conveyor belt to be unloaded in the marshalling area.

Cartons are placed on pallets overtime after having left the conveyor belt. The pallets appear to be placed on the floor randomly, in no apparent order so that halal, non-halal and haram, while generally on different pallets, are placed next to each other. During my visits I did not observe separate personnel handling halal and haram cartons in this area. In one instance I observed a few haram boxes on the same pallet as halal boxes, which were quickly removed as I approached the area where they were located. These practices are most unsatisfactory; they have the potential to undermine Muslim confidence in halal production. There should be a clear demarcation line & separation between halal and haram. A permanent area must be set aside for halal cartons to maintain their integrity. The halal area should also be identified in visible bold writing. This is a most minimum requirement. It is not, however, acceptable to most halal importing Muslim countries that halal cartons are placed in such close proximity to haram and that both are carried on the same conveyor belt. There is no more graphic illustration of how not to produce halal than the way this plant does it at every level.

- The placement of halal and haram pallets in this area is random and close together which makes the possibility of a mix up very high. This in contravention of halal standards

- There is no permanent, separate and identifiable space for halal with appropriate signage.

- The convergence of halal and haram conveyor belts into one towards end of the line is unacceptable. It increases the possibility of mix-up and cross contamination.

Freezer, Chiller and Blasting Areas:

There are two issues to consider in relation to these areas: (1) spatial/ physical separation, and (2) shared air conditioning with haram. Both are matters that are relevant not only to these areas but to the whole ground floor space where production, processing and storage take place. In terms of air conditioning, the question is whether the same airflow for halal and haram in the whole ground floor section or sections within it such as the freezer, chiller etc. contaminates halal products. If the legal *Sharia* opinion is that the halal product in this scenario is contaminated then the issue of separation physical or spatial does not arise. The product is invariably haram and can not be sold to or be consumed by Muslims. If the opinion is the reverse, then it is halal, even though such opinion is most likely to be weak or wrong. What is significant is that the presence of haram at the very least creates doubt, uncertainty and concern about halal status (*Mashbooh*). Muslims are advised in these circumstances to err on the side of caution and avoid the product altogether. This is the most favourable interpretation that can be made in this case. By comparison the majority of learned Muslim opinion is likely to take a more unambiguous view: that is that shared air conditioning such as described above results in contamination of halal products. In other words it is a sufficient condition for the prohibition of these products to be consumed by Muslims.

Independent of the issue of shared air conditioning, separation of halal and haram is under the best conditions difficult to maintain especially when, as in this case, they are being produced in adjoining rooms or in much closer proximity, using the same rails, hooks, personnel and in some circumstances sharing the same confined space. Isolating each room by way of a physical barrier lessens the possibility of physical contact and therefore may address one source of possible contamination but it does not remove other possibilities of contamination altogether.

Conceivably a factory in this and other similar circumstances may be satisfied that the risk of contamination is under control and has been reduced to a manageable proportion. It is reasonable to say however that Islam does not allow for "manageability" of halal in an environment and in circumstances where haram is also produced on a regular basis. A strategic management focused approach that problematises halal and sees it merely as an exercise in problem solving is hardly an approach that shows willingness to embrace a halal ethic. Still it will depend on Muslim majority countries willingness to endorse these practices. But it is highly improbable that they will do so if the conditions such as those in this factory are prevalent.

A Halal Inspection Report of PPP Pty Ltd.*

Spatial separation is difficult to sustain in the production, rail and holding areas as well as on conveyor belts and storage areas. For example there is no demarcation line that separates halal and non-halal in the holding area and in the freezer and chiller area. In fact I have not seen any area designated as an exclusively halal area and no signage to that effect. I have observed non-halal and halal pallets stacked on top of each other.

- Halal, non-halal and haram are all stored together in these areas with minimum separation. Separation however defined is inadequate and unlikely to meet halal standards.

- The shared air conditioning of halal and haram is problematic in these areas and increases the possibility of mix-up and cross contamination.

- Muslim legal opinion is most likely to be of the view that shared air conditioning results in halal contamination.

Supervision and Audit

It appears that there is minimal halal supervision in this factory. There is one halal registered supervisor and no other halal registered workers employed in the factory. This may not be highly unusual for some boning rooms. But the minimum number of registered halal employees should be two- a halal supervisor and a halal process worker- to cover both normal operations and contingencies. However, it is apparent that the supervisor is not properly trained to conduct halal supervision duties. Presumably he is aware of the need for halal separation, in a factory such as this one, where the risk of halal contamination is high to very high. But there is no evidence that he has applied this principle or sought its application in practice. According to the ABC representative who negotiated the transfer of certification from DEF society to ABC society, and the Quality Assurance Officer, the supervisor attends work occasionally even though he is employed fulltime. If true it is astonishing that this is allowed to happen as daily halal production relies totally on his presence and active supervision.

The Australian Quarantine and Inspection service (AQIS) requires that each halal certifying body conduct an audit of halal registered establishments under its auspices every three months. For this purpose it had developed a pro forma audit report document in the form of a check list for certifiers to complete. There is reason to believe that it has become an instrument for some certifiers to avoid performing a proper audit and has encouraged a degree of complacency of simply ticking the designated boxes in the check list, or resubmitting the same report for every audit period. There is serious doubt whether auditing is done properly or done at all in many circumstances. It is obvious that the factory under consideration could not have been audited. If it was, it would not have been allowed to continue halal production in the manner that it currently does.

- There is minimal halal supervision and maximum potential for halal contamination in the plant

- The halal supervisor is not trained to carry out supervision duties and is frequently absent from work

- The audit system appears to have failed; it is unlikely auditing of this establishment has been properly done or done at all

- If auditing was done properly, the plant would not have been allowed to operate

Fundamental Questions of Halal Registration

What is most remarkable about the establishment is that it produces pork, a haram species, in the same premises as it does halal meat. This alone in the eyes of most Muslim authorities-and Muslim consumers-would disqualify it from being fit for halal registration. It is not possible to produce halal in a haram environment (premises) or in an environment where the risk of contamination with haram is high to very high as is the case in this establishment. From a halal perspective the two are mutually

A Halal Inspection Report of PPP Pty Ltd.*

exclusive. It follows therefore that the establishment is in contravention of halal requirements both in terms of fundamental halal principles and prescribed standards and processes. It is also a graphic illustration of the risks associated with co-production of halal and haram meat in the same premises.

Perhaps even more remarkable is that in addition to the plant being a halal registered establishment, there are for that reason, two control officers namely an AQIS inspector and a halal inspector-representing the government and the certifying Islamic society respectively - who oversee halal operations. Each could easily observe that the plant is manifestly far from being halal compliant and cannot legitimately continue to hold halal registration.

These matters raise fundamental questions about how did this establishment (and others like it) obtain halal registration in the first instance, and how did it have its registration renewed over the years? Obviously the system has failed; but the question is how and at what critical points? For example, were the mandatory AQIS halal audits conducted and if they were, why did they not show that halal operations in this establishment are deeply flawed and do not even remotely meet the required halal standard(s)? These are questions beyond my brief and require further investigation to answer them. Control institutions must account for the breakdown of the system in order to prevent its recurrence.

- It is remarkable that this establishment can produce halal and haram in the same premises in the manner that it does and still maintain halal registration as the two are mutually exclusive

- It is also remarkable that the establishment could maintain halal registration under the supervision of an approved Islamic society and AQIS

- These matters raise serious question on why the system failed and at what critical points. Control institutions must account for this failure of the system

Conclusions

No part of this report is intended to reflect in any way negatively on the capacity of this establishment to produce and process meat for sale to non-Muslims or how it manages its operations. In fact I am not qualified to comment on its overall operations except in so far as they pertain to halal food production. This report should therefore be read only in that context.

In so far as halal is concerned the plant's problem is simply that it produces pork- a haram species- in the same premises as it does halal in the manner specified above. The magnitude of this problem in the eyes of Muslims can hardly be overstated. However there is good reason to believe that if the establishment can resolve the pork issue, then it will have little difficulty in meeting halal requirements of Muslim and Muslim majority countries to which Australia exports halal meat. There are four necessary though not sufficient conditions for the establishment to obtain proper halal registration:

1. It must change its halal program to reflect both halal requirements and how the plant will operate in practice
2. It must employ two competent and conscientious supervisors to oversee its daily halal operations
3. The production and storage of pork must be completely removed from the premises and replaced with a halal-only production- this is a primary condition for halal registration
4. Halal production and processes must be validated by an appropriate authority or its representative certifier and reviewed properly thereafter from time to time to maintain Halal integrity

Whatever the weakness ascribed to the establishment are, they merely reflect, to a greater or lesser degree, the weaknesses inherent in the system of halal certification and the "Islamic societies" responsible for it. These societies have a duty of care to their customers- the halal establishments- in not only giving sound advice, but also guiding them through a process, culture and rules they- the customers- may not fully understand. But it is not just halal registered establishments that have difficulty understanding the halal system, many Muslims and halal certifiers

A Halal Inspection Report of PPP Pty Ltd.*

do not fully understand it either-despite their Islamic background and accreditation as certifiers. What this means is that systemic failure is a greater problem than the inability, perceived or real, of an establishment failing to meet prescribed halal standards. Islamic societies must account for these failures if and when they occur. The halal production methods and standards that establishments adopt are as good as the overall system that informs them. That system is largely controlled and implemented by individual Islamic societies in their capacity as halal monitoring, registration and certification societies. The responsibility for any failure in halal compliance is largely theirs.

- The establishment appears to be a well managed entity but it is not in in any way halal compliant.

- Its major problem is simply that it produces Pork in the same premises as it does halal which disqualifies it from being registered as a halal establishment.

- It has the potential to gain halal registration if it becomes a halal only production establishment

Chapter 8

Crisis in Australia's Live Cattle Exports to Indonesia: Where are the Solutions?

A submission to the Senate inquiry into animal welfare standards regarding livestock exports to Indonesia: 10 August 2011

The graphic images of cruelty and mistreatment of Australian cattle exported to Indonesia screened on ABC's Four Corners program on 30 May 2011 were shocking in the extreme. Cruelty to animals is not uncommon in many of the countries to which Australia exports its livestock. Every few years these problems are brought to public attention by investigative programs often relying on evidence provided by animal welfare organisations such as Animal Australia which featured prominently in this program. One may question the motives of some of these groups- or say that their sole purpose is to stop livestock exports- but one can hardly argue with the veracity of the evidence they have presented in this case as in others. Before this incident there were reports of similar problems from the 1990s onwards- in countries such as Kuwait, Saudi Arabia and Egypt, among others. What this tells us is that this is not an isolated problem but a persistent and complex one. What these countries have in common is that they are some of the major importers of Australian livestock; equally importantly they are mainly Muslim or Muslim majority countries. They are also stable trading partners with whom Australia has enjoyed a long, steady and beneficial relationship.

The persistence of the problem is not due to government and industry inaction. Rather it is due to the failure of the actions taken and the strategies adopted to provide the appropriate and desired outcomes. It appears that the government and Industry relied purely on technical instruments- as they always have- to solve the problems associated with cruelty to animals. In the case of Indonesia, they have for example provided purpose-built boxes to restrain cattle during slaughter to participating abattoirs through Meat and Livestock Australia (MLA) - a measure which is now widely accepted to have been deficient in design and implementation. They have also provided a stun and slaughter training program for slaughtermen in these abattoirs. Whatever their shortcomings, these are well-intentioned and important measures. They show the concern Australia has about the treatment of animals it exports. Together these measures may provide some relief even if they do not fully prevent the suffering of animals. Under the appropriate management and control, and in combination with other instruments, they have the potential to improve the conditions under which the cattle are slaughtered, even though this has not been evident from the ABC program. The question is, are they sufficient in themselves to bring about the required solution? It is obvious that they have been unable to do so in isolation. If the recent ABC Four corners program is any guide then it is also clear that these instruments have failed dismally to bring about the mitigation of animal suffering.

Some may argue, and in fact have argued, that the problem is primarily one of implementation- and indeed in part it may well be. If that is the case then the question still remains why has implementation failed consistently over many years? I contend that the key to the solution lies elsewhere, even if implementation is only part of the problem. In order to find a more effective solution one needs to look outside the box of Australia's purely technical remedies. These remedies are basically instructional of dos and don'ts. They are not rooted in or validated by a belief system that sanctions their use and practice; one that justifies and endorses them as having intrinsic values. This is what halal does for Muslims: it is a belief system as well as a world view that validates one's actions and behaviour if they are meritorious and prohibits them if they are morally reprehensible. One can hardly emphasise the value of the concept if what Australia wants to achieve is to entrench the prevention of cruelty to animals in the psyche of those who handle them on a daily basis. I have long argued that Australia should utilise the concept and practice of halal for purposes of trade and commerce, without success. We have heard few passing references to halal in the ABC's Four Corners program. In these instances it was presented as if it was part of the problem not necessarily part of the solution. Certainly it was made clear that it could not offer any solution and therefore deserved no attention. A halal solution was nowhere to be seen in the program. Halal appeared to be anti-stun, anti-reform and at the very least resistant to the treatment of animals in a kind and civilized manner. But nothing could be further from the truth. If Australia wants to see a significant improvement in the treatment of animals in Muslim countries referred to above then it is the view of this writer that it can only achieve this by utilising the halal approach. Australia can not continue to ignore the dominant culture of these countries and yet expect to achieve satisfactory results. We need to grasp the reality that we are operating in halal markets and that the problems that arise may need to a greater or lesser extent a halal approach in resolving them. This has not been the case in this instance or in any other. In fact the tendency has been in Australia to either ignore or minimise the value and efficacy of halal as a strategic tool. However, a solution or a process that is not sanctioned by halal norms particularly in relation to food runs the serious risk of failing to gain traction, widespread acceptance or validation- indeed legitimacy. That is the reason why we should see halal as the key to a permanent solution, not part of the problem as has been the case until now. Over the years government and industry have been tardy and merely reactive in response to concerns about animal welfare. No satisfactory solution has emerged for nearly twenty years. All too often community outrage, led and fanned by the media, is followed by immediate punitive action as in this case and in the case of Egypt where a four year suspension of livestock exports was imposed between 2006 and 2010. But the problems do not go away. They crop up time and again in one Muslim country or another, with no long term solution in sight.

Yet, if there is a will, there is good reason to believe that they can be solved- and more comprehensively than now or in the past.

The technical solutions which Australia has pursued to deal with the problem, sound as they may be in isolation require Indonesian-Muslim norms and values to underpin them in order to gain traction and widespread acceptance. This is why we should embrace halal rules to create the sufficient conditions needed to entrench and normalise the technical solutions. Halal is the embodiment of Islamic culture and values. It enjoins Muslims to be kind to animals and to treat them well. Far from condoning mistreatment of animals, Halal rules require that slaughter must be conducted in a way that causes least distress, pain and suffering to the animal. The halal standard insists in particular on using a very sharp knife; so sharp in fact that killing ought to be performed in one swift, uninterrupted movement. It is almost apologetic in performing the act of slaughter, requiring the slaughterman to do so by invoking God's blessing and acknowledging that the animal's life is about to be taken solely for human sustenance. Even the tools for slaughter must not be exposed to the animal, in order not to cause distress, such that the knife being used for the kill must be hidden from its view. Many Muslim countries have also in recent times validated stunning before slaughter as an acceptable Islamic practice, mainly on the grounds that it does mitigate animal suffering- even though the question of whether stun or slaughter causes more or less suffering to the animal remains unresolved. These are humane values. Indonesia subscribes to them. It behoves Australia to utilise them to deal with the problems of mistreatment of animals in Muslim countries, as it is the most effective way to achieve the desired results. It is possible to develop and utilise our own halal rules or develop a common framework with Indonesia to address issues of concern. This approach would require us to think outside the box; outside that is the frame of reference to which we are accustomed. This is likely to unsettle those with a mindset that can not conceive of solutions outside the norm of Australian rules. To operationalize this approach needs working closely and cooperatively with Indonesians and/or with Australian Muslim leaders and experts. I am willing to discuss how this approach might be developed, structured and made to work.

The presumption underlying the ABC program is that Indonesians on the whole are horribly unkind to animals and unsympathetic to their welfare. It seemed to imply that the culture sanctions mistreatment or at least condones it. It did not explore ideas or alternatives on how to solve this issue and other broader related issues. Uncompromisingly strident in its criticism, it did not advance cooperation with the Indonesian government as an avenue worth pursuing. Instead it urged or seemed to favour punitive action. Unfortunately Australian government's reaction was too accommodating, swift and irreversible, with the Minister for Agriculture signing "a ban on 12 facilities in Indonesia which came into law at midnight... [Thursday 2 June 2011]". The media had called for bans and penalties if not for the termination of the cattle trade to Indonesia, to which Minister responded positively. The decision and the media campaign smack of both moral righteousness and hypocrisy at the same time. It was also an act of desperation to do something in order to silence criticism. Indonesia is not the only country to which Australia exports livestock where such practices can be found and the government knows it, and so do the media. If we carry this policy to its logical conclusion we might as well decide to have no livestock exports to our trading partners, including Indonesia. But we know that will not be done and perhaps can not be done, without inflicting considerable economic and social costs on Australians. Australia needs to export livestock to Indonesia more than Indonesia needs to import them. This hardline approach is counterproductive. It does not seem to be about finding a solution at all but about abandoning the search for one. The trouble with this approach is that it does not look outside the box of purely technical solutions. It does not see Indonesia as having the capacity much less the desire to act- which is patently false. This is a dangerous view to take in trade and commerce and it may have broader implications for the relations between Australia and Indonesia if the arguments of the ABC program and the conclusions drawn from it are accepted as sound policy prescriptions. Australians (and no less the Indonesians) ought to be horrified by the maltreatment of animals in Indonesia or anywhere else it occurs- and not just for the animals Australia exports. But we must not allow Australia's vital national interests to be swayed, by a highly emotive program whose intentions- however good they may be- have the potential to damage Australia's relations with the people and government of Indonesia.

Glossary

The terms in this glossary are used as they are generally understood by ordinary Muslims.

Al Quran (Quran)	The Holy book of Islam revealed by Allah to the Prophet Mohammad, Peace be upon Him (PBUH) through the Angel Gabriel
Asl -	denotes origin, source, foundation, principle or nature
Bida'	means innovation or unapproved innovation, suggesting divergence from Islamic tradition
Fatwa	A legal opinion given by a mufti or religious authority
Fiqh -	Islamic jurisprudence (the science of Islamic law)
Halal certificate	a document that validates products as having a Halal status or having met a Halal standard and accompanies them to their export destination or sales outlet
Halal Interim/ Transfer certificate	A Halal certificate that accompanies the movement and storage of Halal products to maintain their Halal integrity

Halal program	a mandatory program to be submitted by a business enterprise to a halal authority or its representative to show how it will comply or how it complies with a prescribed Halal standard in order gain Halal approval for its products and maintain Halal registration for its premises
GCC countries	Gulf Cooperation Council countries comprising, Saudi Arabia, the UAE, Qatar, Bahrain, Kuwait and Oman
Halal	food or activity that is legally permitted in Islamic law
Halal standard(s)	A set of *Sharia* based principles, rules and values which Halal registered establishment ought to comply with to be able to produce Halal goods and services
Haram	Food or activity that is prohibited in Islamic law
Ibadaat	Acts of worship of Allah
ICCA	Islamic Coordinating Council of Victoria- A halal certification organisation in Melbourne (now defunct)
Majelis Ulama Indonesia (MUIS):	The top Muslim clerical body in Indonesia which is also the authority responsible for management and control of Halal food.
Khamar	Alcohol
Kosher	Food that is fit for consumption according to Jewish law
Madahib	Schools of law referring to the four schools of law in Islam (singular Mad'hab)
Makrooh	That which is hateful in the eyes of Allah but is nonetheless legally permitted
Mashbooh	Food or activity that is doubtful as Halal and must be avoided by Muslims
Muamalaat	An individual's relationship with other human beings and with the environment around him/her

Glossary

Mohammad (peace be Upon Him (PBUH))	The Prophet of Islam and as Muslims believe of all mankind.
Nejis	Unclean, filth
Non-Halal	Products that are in origin Halal but are rendered not Halal in the process of making, handling, moving or storing them
PBUH	Peace be upon him, a reverential term which commonly accompanies the mention of the Prophet Mohammed and any of the Prophets before him including Moses and Jesus (Peace be upon them)
Sharia	Islamic Law
Sunna	The traditions of the Prophet Mohammad (PBUH)
Ulama (or Ulema)	The body of Muslim scholars who are trained in Islamic law (singular alim)

References

Chapter 1

Agriculture and Agri-Food Canada 2007,*Global Halal Food Market July 2007*, <www.ats-sea.agr.gc.ca/afr/4352-eng.htm>. p.1; viewed 19 May2010.

Agriculture and Agri-Food Canada 2011,*Global Halal Food Market May 2011*, <www.ats-sea.agr.gc.ca/afr/4352-eng.htm>. p.2, viewed 28 April 2011.

Al-Katheeri, H.S 1996, "Food labelling: A tool to promote the marketing of processed foods". *Proceedings: First International Halal Food Conference,* Arabic Society of Victoria, Melbourne, p. 29

Al Qaradawi, Y. Undated, *The Lawful and the Prohibited in Islam*, translated by El-Helbawy and others. Hindustan Publications, Delhi: 15-17, 21, 35-36, 31-33

Al-Quran Al-Kareem, 1934, (Translated by Abdullahi Yusuf Ali), Dar El Arabia, Beirut, 5:4, 2:219.

Aus-Meat 1999, Malaysian Approved Establishment List. Aus-Meat Australia.

Giles, M 1996, "Satisfying consumer demand: key to Bonlac's success in halal markets", *Proceedings: First International Halal Food Conference*, Arabic Society of Victoria, Melbourne, p. 116.

ICCA (Islamic Coordinating Council of Australia) 1997, *Halal Food Procedures and Processes: A Guide*, Melbourne.

Pew Research Centre January 2011, *The future of the Global Muslim Population: projections for 2010-2030*, <http://pewresarch.org/pubs/1872/muslim-population-projections-w0>. P.1, viewed 7 March 2012.

SMO (Standardization and Metrology Organisation for GCC Countries) 1984, *Labelling of Prepackaged Foods*, Saudi Arabian Government Document Riyadh, cited in ICCA records.

Chapter 2

Agriculture and Agi-Food Canada 2007,*Global Halal Food Market July 2007*, <www.ats-sea.agr.gc.ca/afr/4352-eng.htm>. p.1; 1, viewed 19 May 2010.

Agriculture and Agi-Food Canada 2011,*Global Halal Food Market May 2011*, <www.ats-sea.agr.gc.ca/afr/4352-eng.htm>. p.2;2, viewed 28 April 2011.

Al-Katheeri Hassan Saeed 1996, "Food labeling: A tool to promote the marketing of processed foods" *Proceedings First International Halal Food Conference (INHAFCON 96)*, Arabic Society of Victoria Melbourne, pp. 31-33.

Yusuf Al Qardawi undated, *The lawful and the Prohibited in Islam*, Hindustan Publications India, p.14; 32-33; 26.

Girindra Aisjah 1996,"The Problems of Food Additives in Indonesia's Halal Food", *Proceedings First International Halal Food Conference (INHAFCON 96)*, Arabic Society of Victoria Melbourne 1996, p.122.

Halal Research Council circa 2006, *Development of the Halal Industry*, Chapter 21, <http://www.halalrc.org/images/researchmaterial/literature/developmentofhalalfood.pdf>, pp. 953-94, viewed 17 March 2012.

Hamid Jafaar Dato M. 2008, "Opportunities and Strategies in Halal Market: [A] Brunei Perspective". Paper delivered at Singapore International Halal Conference, pp.7-8.

Meat and Livestock Australia (MLA), *International Marketing*, <http://www.mla.com.au/marketing-red-meat/>, p.1-2, viewed 7 March 2012.

Meat and Livestock Australia (MLA), *Red Meat Markets: Middle East*, <www.mla.com.au/topichierarchy/marketinginformation/>, p.4; p.4; viewed 17 May 2010.

Pew Research Center January 2011, *The future of the Global Muslim Population: Projections for 2010-2030*, p.1-2; p. 1-2. < http://pewresearch.org/ > viewed 7 March 2012.

Soesilowati Endang S 2010, "Business Opportunities for Halal Products in the Global Market: Muslim Consumer Behaviour and Halal Food Consumption", *Journal of Indonesian Social Science and*

Humanities, vol. 3, 2010 p.151 <www.kitlv-journals.nl/index.php/>, p.1; 1; viewed 17 March 2012.

United States Department of Agriculture 2010, *International Meat Review 21 January 2010*, < www.themeatsite.com/articles/867/international>, viewed 25 May 2010, sourced from the Australian Department of Agriculture Fisheries and Forestry.

Chapter 4

Al Katheeri, Hassan saeed 1996, "Food Labelling: A tool to Promote the Marketing of Processed Food in Muslim Countries", *First International Halal Food Conference (INHAFCON 96)*, Arabic Society of Victoria, Melbourne, Pp.32-33; 33.

Abd al Ati, Hammuda 1977, *The Family Structure in Islam*, American Trust Publications, Brentwood, Maryland, p.13 (quoted from Shorter Encyclopedia of Islam eds. H.A.R. Gibb and Kramer, J.H.Leiden: E.Brill 1953) pp. 14; 14,

Al Qardawi, Yusuf undated, *The Lawful and the prohibited in Islam*, Hindustan Publications, India, p.33

Al Quran (2:29); (45:13); (31:20); (5:5); (5:6); (20:81); (2:219); (5.4, 5.3); (5:90-91), (87-88). I am indebted to Dr. Qardawi for these references in the Quran and his analysis which I have relied on.

Girindra, Aisjah 1996, The Problems of Food Additives in Indonesia's Halal Food, *First International Halal Food Conference (INHAFCON 96)*, Arabic Society of Victoria Melbourne p.122.

Grunebaum, Gustave E. von 1953, *Medieval Islam*, The University of Chicago (2nd ed.), p. 144.

Halal Research Council, (circa 2006), *Development of the Halal Industry*, chapter 1, <www.halalrc.org/ > pp.953-54 viewed 17 March 2012.

Hamid, Jafaar Dato M. 2008, "Opportunities and Strategies in Halal Market: [A] Brunei Perspective". Paper delivered at Singapore International Halal Conference, pp.8; 8; 5-7. Author has a copy.

Hussaini, Mohammad Mazhar 1993, *Islamic Dietary Concepts and Practices*, Islamic Food and Nutrition Council of America, Bedford Park Illinois, p.27.

Rodinson, Maxime 2007, *Islam and Capitalism*, Saqi Books, London p.64.

Soesilowati, Endang S 2010, "Business Opportunities for Halal Products in the global market: Muslim Consumer Behaviour and Halal Food Consumption" *Journal of Indonesian Social Sciences and Humanities* vol.3, 2010, p.151, viewed 17March 2012, <www.kitlv-journals.nl/index.php/>. This estimate of the expected rate of growth of halal trade is attributed to President Yudhoyono of Indonesia in a speech he gave at the third World Islamic economic Conference in K.L. Malaysia 2007.

Chapter 5

'Abd al 'Ati, Hammudah 1977, *The Family Structure in Islam*, American Trust Publications, Indianapolis, pp. 15-16.

Agriculture and Agri-Food Canada (July 2007), "Global Halal Food Market", <http://www.ats.agr.gc.ca/inter/4352-eng.htm> , p.1; 1, viewed 19 May 2010.

Al Qardawy, Yusuf (Sheikh) undated, *The Lawful and the Prohibited in Islam*, Hindustan Publications, Delhi, pp. 37; 29-32; 15-17, 33-36.

Al Quran (2:137).

Australian Parliament 2004, Proof Committee Hansard, Inquiry into "Expanding Australia's Trade & Investment Relationship with the Economies of the Gulf States", hearing of evidence, 7 April 2004, pp.16-17. Copy with author.

Ayan, Abdullahi 2001, "Halal Food with Specific Reference to Australian Exports", *Food Australia* Vol. 53, No.11, pp.498-499.

Balmer, John 2006, "Corporate brand Cultures", in Schroder, J. et.al. (eds.) *Brand Culture*, Taylor and Francis, London, pp. 41, 38 and 34.

Danesi, Marcel. (2006), *Brands*, Francis and Taylor, New York, pp. 14 and 97.

Hamid, Jaafar Dato M 2007, " Opportunities and Strategies in Halal market: Brunei Perspective", *Paper delivered at the First Singapore International Halal Showcase,* pp. 8; 8; 5-7; 2.

Hindess, Barry 1986, Interests in Political Analysis, in Laws, J. (ed.), *Power, Action and Belief: A New Sociology of Knowledge*, Routledge and Keagan Paul, London, p. 120.

Interbrand 1991, *Brands: An International Review*, Mercury Books, London, p.12.

See Lapidus, Ira 1988, *A History of Islamic Societies*, Cambridge University Press, pp. 573- 580 on issue of quietism.

Ministry of Industry & Primary Resources 2008 "Guideline for Use of the Brunei Halal Brand" <http://www.industry.gov.bn/webservices/bruneihalal/doc/Guideline> viewed 15 May 2008.

Nahan, M 2003, "Don't Give in to Brand-Mail: Green Groups are Attacking Companies they Don't Like", The *Australian Financial Review* < www.afr.com>, 28 August 2003, p.63.

Parratt, C. and Holloway, K. (1990), "The Value of Brands" in Power, M. (ed.), *Brand and Goodwill Accounting Strategies*, Simon and Schuster, Cambridge, p.42.

Peattie, K. (2007), "Sustainable Marketing: Marketing Re-thought, Re-mixed and Re-tooled" in Saren M. et al. *Critical Marketing: Defining the field*, Butterworth-Heinemann, Oxford, pp.201-202.

Pew Research Center January 2011, *The Future if the Global Muslim Population: Projections for 2010-2030*, <http://pewresearch.org/pubs/>, p.1; 1.

Power, M 1992, "The Politics of Brand Accounting in the United Kingdom", *The European Accounting Review*, Vol. 1, issue 1, pp.41-43, main ideas in this section have drawn on this work.

Report of the Royal Commission into the Australian Meat Industry 1982, AGPS Canberra, See also my report: (2003), "Islamic societies that monitor and certify halal meat in Australia: A framework for reform".

Sheridan, N 2007, "Victorians work on first global halal brand", *The Age*, 24 September 2007, where it is reported that 200 manufacturers and producers are working with government of Brunei to develop the world's first halal brand.

Soesilowati Endang 2010, "Business Opportunities for Halal Products in the Global Market: Muslim Consumer behaviour and Halal Food Consumption", *Journal of Indonesian Social Science and*

Humanities, vol. 3, 2010, p.1, <www.kitlv-lournals.nl/index.php/>, viewed 17 May 2012.

Wheeler, A 2003, *Designing Brand Identity*, John Wiley, New York, p.2, also quoted in Danesi, p.8.

Tawney, RH (1954), *Religion and the Rise of Capitalism*, Harcourt, Brace and World, New York, p.9.

The Age 2008, "Controversial Pulp Mill to Go Ahead, Despite ANZ Snub" 30 May 2008.

The Economist 2004, "Political Food: Mullah moolah", 30 October 2004 also in Balmer, p. 41.

Appendices

Appendix 1 Uncompleted halal certificate

ORIGINAL	بسم الله الرحمن الرحيم (شهادة بالذبيح على الطريقة الاسلامية) **(Certificate for Meat Slaughtered by Muslims)**	XXXXXX
Name of Islamic Organisation		**Stamp**
Signature of Representative		

يشهد المؤسسة الاسلامية الموضح اسمها أعلاه بأن ارسالية هذه اللحوم البينه ادناه نحو حيوانات نبحت على يد ذباح مسلم تحت اشراف هذه المؤسسة طبقا للشريعة الاسلامية وبذلك فلحوم هذه الحيوانات صالحة لاستهلاك المسلمين في جميع أنحاء العالم. وقد اتخذت كافة الاجرءات اللازمة لعدم اختلاطها بلحوم أخرى.

The Islamic Organisation certifies that the consignment of meat detailed below is from animals slaughtered by Muslim slaughtermen, authorised by the Organisation, using a knife and according to Islamic rites. The meat of animals so slaughtered is Halal and therefore suitable for consumption by Muslims in any part of the World. Adequate precautions have been taken to prevent mixing with non-Halal meat.

Description of meat	Official Mark
Marks	
t mass	
Ship/voyage or Airline/flight	
Port/airport	**Australian Government** Department of Agriculture, Fisheries and Forestry Australian Quarantine and Inspection Service
Abattoir/works	
I hereby certify that since the meat specified in this certificate became Halal at the time of slaughter by a Muslim slaughterman authorised by the above Islamic organisation, it has not lost its identity nor become mixed with non-halal meat	**Government Seal**
Date of issue	
Place of issue In the State of	

Appendix 2 Completed Interim/Transfer certificate

Islamic Co-ordinating Council Of Australia Inc
Reg. No. A0032009W

INTERIM* \TRANSFER**CERTIFICATE

I, the undersigned, hereby certify that the consignment of meat / food detailed below is slaughtered by me / processed under my supervision as a Muslim slaughterman / Inspector according to Islamic rites. Adequate precautions have been taken to prevent mixing Halal products with non Halal.

* Interim certificate to be completed when an official Halal certificate (Ex237-690) is required.
** Transfer certificate to be completed when Halal products shipped from one place to another in Australia.

INTERIM CERTIFICATE

Description: 104 Chilled bone-in lamb carcases

Mark: NIL
Net Mass: 1402 KGS
Ship / Airline / Flight: TG999 (50) of 30.9.01
Final Destination: MUSCAT
Air: ES - 612
Norvic Food Processing
Slaughtering Date: 28-9-2001
Packaging / Processing Date: 28-9-2001

Work Manager: M o Cxleir
Signature: Mintop JC
ICCV's Personnel: NABIL HAMIE
ID No.: 162
Signature: NABIL HAMIE

TRANSFER CERTIFICATE

Despatched to:
Date:
Description   Qty.   Weight

OK

Abattoir / Boning Room / Cold Store / Processing Plant:
Date Slaughter / Transfer / Process:
Truck / Container No.:
Seal No.:   Sup. Seal No. (if required):
Certificate Number: 25000
Received by at Boning Room, Cold Storage:
ICCV's Personnel:
ID No.:   Date:
Signature:
Seal No.:

Interim / Transfer certificate not for official use or export purposes.   IT-F390

155 Lygon Street, East Brunswick, Vic. 3057 Tel: (03) 9380 5467 Fax: (03) 9380 6143

Appendices

Appendix 3 Newspaper article on questionable halal certification

Bunfight over halal burgers

Whopping mystery — it's time for a flame grilling

Food | Paige Mason

AN authority that certifies halal food in Victoria is standing by its practices amid a bunfight between a fast food giant and its franchisee.

Hungry Jack's is investigating its Tullamarine restaurant after reports it was selling halal food.

It is also seeking clarification from the Islamic Coordinating Council of Victoria (ICCV) how certification was obtained.

ICCV gave the Tullamarine restaurant its certification on December 31 last year.

ICCV administration manager Sidki Guzem said an inspector visited the Tullamarine store and the council was "100 per cent" confident in its checks.

But confusion remains in the Muslim community about whether the food was in fact halal.

Hungry Jack's Australia chief executive Aaron McKie said halal-certified items have never been available from any of their restaurants.

"No halal product was supplied to the restaurant by any of Hungry Jack's approved suppliers," Mr McKie said.

But Tullamarine franchisee Nicholas Raptis said he had not misled customers in any way.

"I do buy all my products from Hungry Jack's and am proud to be a Hungry Jack's store owner," Mr Raptis said.

"We supply all the food Hungry Jack's supply."

Hungry Jack's has asked the franchisee to explain how the certification was obtained.

"The company is still trying to establish the chain of events which led to ICCV awarding a halal certificate to the restaurant," Mr McKie said.

He said the franchisee made unauthorised claims and breached the trust of customers and the company.

Hungry Jack's has contacted ICCV to clarify how the restaurant had received a halal certificate.

Mr Guzem said the council checked suppliers to see where the meat was coming from and whether it had halal certification.

"We do check the records, we make sure the meat is halal and from halal sources," Mr Guzem said.

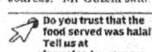
Do you trust that the food served was halal?
Tell us at
humeleader.com.au

Halal means meat needs to be cut by a Muslim invoking the name of god, before killing the animal with a sharp knife, rather than stunning the animal.
NIAL AYKEN, Islamic Council Victoria general manager

Courtesy of: Leader Community Newspapers and reporter, Paige Mason

Appendix 4 Instant noodle brand (Indomie) with proper certification

Appendices

Appendix 5 Top: Cover design of Coon cheese brand obscuring halal inscription below; Bottom: halal inscription on Coon cheese slices without source of approval

Australians don't say cheese, they say COON.
After all, Australians have been enjoying
COON for over 70 years. With its full flavour
and tangy taste, it's no wonder COON
is Australia's Tastiest Cheese.

Accessing the Global Halal Market

Appendix 6 List of approved halal certifiers of red meat in Australia

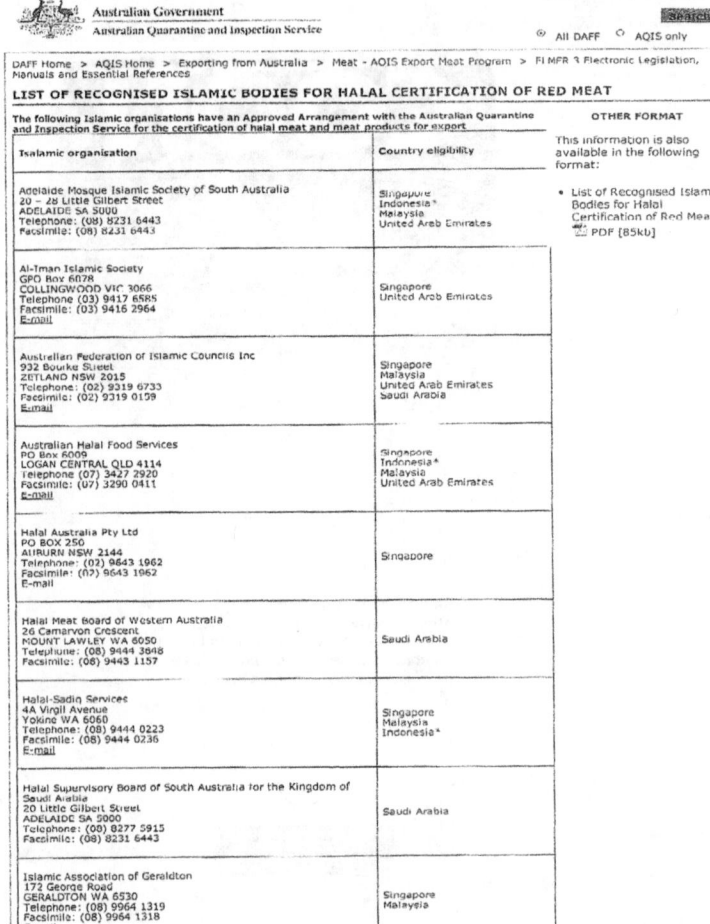

Appendices

list of recognised islamic bodies for halal certification of red meat ...   http://www.daff.gov.au/aqis/export/meat/elmer-3/list-islamic-halal...

Isalamic organisation	Country eligibility
Islamic Association of Katanning PO Box 270 KATANNING WA 6317 Telephone: 0429 940 113 Facsimile: (08) 9821 2731 E-mail	Singapore Indonesia* Malaysia United Arab Emirates
Islamic Coordinating Council of Victoria PO Box 108 EAST BRUNSWICK VIC 3057 Telephone: (03) 9380 5467 Facsimile: (03) 9380 6143 E-mail	Singapore Indonesia* Malaysia United Arab Emirates Saudi Arabia
Islamic Council of Western Australia PO Box 70 BURSWOOD WA 6100 Telephone: (08) 9362 2210 Facsimile: (08) 9362 2210 E-mail	Singapore Indonesia* Malaysia
Perth Mosque Incorporated 26 Camarvon Crescent MOUNT LAWLEY WA 6050 Telephone: (08) 9444 3648 Facsimile: (08) 9443 1157	Singapore Indonesia* Malaysia United Arab Emirates
Supreme Islamic Council of Halal Meat in Australia Inc Unit 1/35-37 Harrow Road AUBURN NSW 2144 Telephone: (02) 9643 7775 Facsimile: (02) 9643 7776 E-mail	Singapore Indonesia* Malaysia United Arab Emirates Saudi Arabia

*IMPORTANT: certification of slaughter requires Islamic organisations who are listed for Indonesia to only provide this service in the State or Region the organisation is located.

Contact: Email AQIS Export Meat Program   Last reviewed: 19 Apr 2010
             About AQIS and Contact details
             Media inquiries

© Commonwealth of Australia 2010

Appendix 7 Halal operational manual (halal program) of a halal approved establishment

Australian Government Supervised Muslim Slaughter
Standard Operating Procedure

CRF (Colac Otway) Pty Ltd
Issued on: *3 June 2009*
Department: *Technical Services*
SOP: *AGSMS*

Controlled Copy No: 1
Revision No: 1
Amendment No.: 3
Page 1 of 11

Appendices

AMENDMENT REGISTER

AMEND-MENT No.	ISSUE DATE	AMENDED SECTION	AMENDMENT DESCRIPTION	AUTHORISED BY
1	24/02/09		• All references to ICCV have been removed & inserted Australian Halal Food services.	S. Barrow
2	23/04/09		• Amended AGSMS process checklist, inserted 'MTC states non Halal carcase on board?' deleted stun reversibility section.	S. Barrow
3	03/06/09	1.5.3	• Removed 'ONLY "HALAL" eligible carcases shall be boned in the Boning room.' • Inserted 'If "non HALAL" carcase/s are to be boned in the further processing room, an Authorised Muslim Slaughterman must be notified prior to the carcase/s entering the room as an Authorised Muslim Slaughterman must be present to supervise the process. • The "non HALAL" carcase/s are subject to normal boning procedures but are segregated from normal boning lines, are packed separately & stored at Otway Fresh in the designated 'non HALAL" area.	S. Barrow
			•	
			•	
			•	

Issued on: 3 June 2009
Department: Technical Services
SOP: AGSMS

Controlled Copy No: 1
Revision No: 1
Amendment No: 3
Page 2 of 11

183

AMENDMENT REGISTER

AMENDMENT No.	ISSUE DATE	AMENDED SECTION	AMENDMENT DESCRIPTION	AUTHORISED BY
1	24/02/09		• All references to ICCV have been removed & inserted Australian Halal Food services.	S. Barrow
2	23/04/09		• Amended AGSMS process checklist, inserted 'MTC states non Halal carcase on board?' deleted stun reversibility section.	S. Barrow
3	03/06/09	1.5.3	• Removed 'ONLY "HALAL" eligible carcases shall be boned in the Boning room.' • Inserted 'If "non HALAL" carcase/s are to be boned in the further processing room, an Authorised Muslim Slaughterman must be notified prior to the carcase/s entering the room as an Authorised Muslim Slaughterman must be present to supervise the process. • The "non HALAL" carcase/s are subject to normal boning procedures but are segregated from normal boning lines, are packed separately & stored at Otway Fresh in the designated 'non HALAL" area.	S. Barrow
			•	
			•	
			•	

Issued on: 3 June 2009
Department: Technical Services
SOP: AGSMS

Controlled Copy No: 1
Revision No: 1
Amendment No: 3

Appendices

1 AGSMS APPROVED PROGRAM

1.1 Purpose
To outline and describe the implementation and operation of the "HALAL" Program at CRF (Colac-Otway) Pty Ltd, Establishment Number 0282.

1.2 Scope
This program covers the identification, slaughter, chilling/freezing, further processing & loading of "HALAL" product in accordance with Schedule 7 of the Export Control (Meat & Meat Product) Orders 2005. Species covered by this program include Lamb, Mutton, and Calves.
The Islamic organisation, recognised by AQIS and AUSMEAT, & used by CRF (Colac Otway) Pty Ltd., is the, Australian Halal Food Services, PO Box 250, Springwood QLD 4127.

1.2.1 Key Responsibilities

Position	Responsibilities
Export Standards Manager	• Overall responsibility for the program. • Conducting verification activities.
Export Standards Co-ordinator	• System development & maintenance. • Document Control.
Auditor	• Verification activities. • AUS-MEAT OIC. • Review & filing of monitoring & verification documentation.
QA Monitor	• Monitor AGSMS program. • Initiate corrective action.
Managers	• Take corrective action as required. • Ensure procedures are followed. • Track "Non HALAL" carcases from identification to retain chiller.
Dr Mohammed Lotfi	• Australian Halal Food Service rep.
Authorised Muslim Slaughtermen. Refer attachment for names & ID.	• Complying with requirements associated with the slaughter of animals in accordance with the Muslim faith. • Maintaining current registration. • Identification of "Non HALAL" carcases. • "Non HALAL" segregation verification. • Monthly Audit of Completion of Halal Inspection. • Supervising control on "Non HALAL" carcases-Sticking to Retain chiller.

Issued on: 3 June 2009 Ltd
Department: Technical Services
SOP: AGSMS

Controlled Copy No: 1
Revision No: 1
Amendment No: 3

Accessing the Global Halal Market

1.3 References

- Export Control (Meat & Meat Product) Orders 2005.
- Certification requirements of the Australian Halal Food Services (AHFS)
- Export Control (Prescribed Goods – General) Orders.
- AQIS Meat Notices: 1999/17 – Animal welfare explanatory notes & stunning.
  2002/16 – AGSMS – Halal program
  2003/11 – Non defacement of the official halal mark
- The list of recognised Islamic bodies for halal certification of red meat, accessed through ELMER 3 Electronic Legislation, Manuals and Essential References - DAFF
- WI-PF-1&2

1.4 Definitions

Approved Program	An approved program is a contractual agreement between the Establishment management and AQIS that describes the manner in which Establishment management will satisfy legislative requirements relevant to a specific operation addressed in the program
AQIS OPVO	Australian Quarantine and Inspection Service On Plant Veterinary Officer
AQIS ATM	Area Technical Manager
AHFS	Australian Halal Food Services
AMS	Authorised Muslim Slaughterman

Appendices

1.5 Procedures

1.5.1 Stunning/Sticking procedures

- Authorised Muslim Slaughterers (AMS) are those who are a member of AHFS & possesses a current identity card issued by AUS-MEAT.
- All animals are stunned by way of an electrical stunning device. The head only stun must not be fatal. Reversibility of stun is checked when requested & taking into consideration Animal welfare issues. See Stun Reversibility checklist.
- Stock must be stuck within 15 seconds of stunning for lambs & 10 seconds for calves.
- The animal is stuck by the AMS using a single cut which severs the trachea, weasand & all other major blood vessels in the neck. Dressing does not commence until the animal is dead.
- Standard hygiene & sanitation procedures are followed by AMS during processing operations.
- "HALAL" carcases are branded with the "HALAL" brand between the carcase wash & the carcase chillers.

1.5.2 Non Halal product

- All processing at CRF is in accordance with "HALAL" slaughter requirements.
- **Carcases may be designated by the AMS as not eligible for "HALAL" Meat.** Carcases identified as "non HALAL" shall be tagged with a yellow ticket bearing the words "Non HALAL" by the AMS. This ticket will then be transferred to the carcase gambrel.
- Two spaces following a "non HALAL" carcase will be provided to prevent carcase contact.
- "Non HALAL" carcases are tracked to the retain chiller by an AMS and or manager. In the event that a "non HALAL" carcase is condemned by AQIS it will be held on the condemn rail to allow for the AMS to verify.
- CRF operators, under direction of either the manager or an AMS condemn offal from a carcase identified as "non HALAL" on the processing floor.
- "Non HALAL" carcases will be held in the retain chiller on a separate rail from that of HALAL carcases and the retain chiller will be secured.
- The "non HALAL" carcase ticket will remain attached to the carcase until load out.
- If the Manager cannot be present the AMS will stop the chain.

1.5.3 Further processing

- "HALAL" carcases are identified with the "HALAL" brand.
- If "non HALAL" carcase/s are to be boned in the further processing room, an Authorised Muslim Slaughterman must be notified prior to the carcase/s entering the room as an Authorised Muslim Slaughterman must be present to supervise the process.
- The "non HALAL" carcase/s are subject to normal boning procedures but are segregated from normal boning lines, are packed separately & stored at Otway Fresh in the designated 'non HALAL" area.
- Product destined for the "HALAL" market will be identified with the application of the "HALAL" brand to the end panel of the carton.

Issued on: 3 June 2009
Department: Technical Services
SOP: AGSMS

Controlled Copy No: 1
Revision No: 1
Amendment No.: 3
Page 6 of 11

Accessing the Global Halal Market

1.5.4 Storage & Load out
- All Chilled/frozen Product branded and held on plant is "HALAL" product and thus no separation is necessary in carton storage.
- "Non – HALAL" carcases will be held in the retain chiller on a separate rail from that of "HALAL" carcases and the retain chiller will be secured. "Non –HALAL" carcases will be loaded out for the domestic market the next day they will remain separate from "HALAL" eligible carcases during and after loading.

1.5.5. Transportation of "HALAL" product
- Product is identified as "HALAL" (Australia MS stamp) before load out.
- If product "HALAL" status is lost then "VIC MS" stamp is defaced or removed.
- Transportation in the event of mixed loads, all "HALAL" product leaving Est. 282 shall be physically segregated from "non – HALAL" product by using a plastic sheet barrier.
- The MTC must be endorsed to indicate **"HALAL MEAT"** is on the vehicle.

1.5.6 HALAL Documentation
- The AMS is responsible for the issuing of the Interim "HALAL" documentation.
- "HALAL" certificates are issued & copies returned to the QA office for filing.

1.5.7 Control of HALAL brands
- AQIS personnel keep a daily register for the issuing and return of "VIC MS" brand. Brands will only be released to designated responsible company personnel. The brands are kept under AQIS security.

1.5.8 Monitoring
- Monitoring of the program is through the established MHA process monitoring system.

1.5.9 Verification
- The contents of this procedure are subjected to internal audit at least once per year.
- The process is reviewed on a quarterly basis by the AMS.
- Monitoring records are reviewed by the Technical Services department on a daily basis.
- Adverse trends that cannot be corrected without executive assistance will be submitted to the Management Review process which is conducted at 4 monthly intervals.

1.5.10 Corrective Action
- A CRF System Improvement Notice (SIN) will be immediately raised at any time deviation from this program is detected.
- All corrective action will be detailed on the reverse side of the MHA process monitoring form & CRF SIN.
- If "HALAL" status of product is lost then all possibly affected product will also lose its "HALAL" status.

Issued on: 3 June 2009
Department: Technical Services
SOP: AGSMS

Appendices

1.6 Documentation
- Process floor process monitoring form
- Further Processing process monitoring form
- Load out process monitoring form
- Internal audit reports
- "HALAL" Checklist
- Management review minutes
- Cold Storage monitoring form

Issued on: 3 June 2009
Department: Technical Services
SOP: AGSMS

Controlled Copy No: 1
Revision No: 1
Amendment No.: 3
Page 8 of 11

Appendix 1

AUTHORISED MUSLIM SLAUGHTERER - *AHFS Registration*

Appendices

Resemblance of MS brand used at CRF (Colac Otway) Pty Ltd.

Issued on: *3 June 2009*
Department: *Technical Services*
SOP: *AGSMS*

Controlled Copy No: 1
Revision No: 1
Amendment No.: 3
Page 10 of 11

Accessing the Global Halal Market

AGSMS Process Checklist

Stock class: Lamb ☐   Sheep ☐   Calf ☐

Ref.	Requirement	Met? (☑☒)	Comment or action
1.2	Scope covers relevant processes?		
1.2.4	Responsibilities current?		
1.5.1	Muslim slaughters registered?		
	Amp / voltage requirements OK?		
	Stick within 10 for calves & 15 seconds for lambs of stun?		
	Carcases branded with MS stamp?		
1.5.2	"Non HALAL" tickets available & used?		
	Space each side of a "Non HALAL" carcase?		
	"Non HALAL" offal condemned?		
	"Non HALAL" carcases in retain chiller?		
1.5.3	Only "HALAL" carcases boned?		
	"HALAL" carcases branded?		
	"HALAL" cartons branded?		
1.5.5	"HALAL" product properly branded at load out?		
	Segregation of mixed loads?		
	MTC states non Halal carcase on board?		
1.5.7	Brands controlled by AQIS?		

Signed by Authorised Slaughterman: .... Date: ....

Issued on: *3 June 2009*
Department: *Technical Services*
SOP: *AGSMS*

Controlled Copy No: 1
Revision No: 1
Amendment No.: 3

Index

Abattoirs, xxi, xxii, 7–10, 12, 39, 40, 42, 43, 75, 79, 160
ABC (Australia Broadcasting commission) T.V program, 160, 162–3
ABC (Islamic) society, 143–5, 153
Access (to market),xvii, 20, 25, 32, 35, 40, 43–4, 46
Accountability, 52, 61, 129, 132, 142
Accreditation, xi, 7–8, 28–9, 31–2, 49, 51–3, 82, 88, 114, 128–35, 138, 141,157
Agent(s), 7, 87, 98, 118
Agriculture and Agri–Food Canada, 5, 6, 17–18, 67, 96–7, 169, 172
Alcohol, xii, 4–5, 73, 79–81, 126, 138, 166
Allegro Pty Ltd., 12
Al Qardawi, Yusuf, xv, 16, 18, 74, 76, 97, 114, 170–1
Al Quran, xiii, xx, 2, 4–6, 71–6, 81, 113, 165, 169, 171–2
Animal welfare, xxi, 4, 159, 161
Arabic, xviii, 29, 31, 71, 94, 117, 169–70
Asl, 16, 25–6, 81, 84–5, 113, 165
Attribute, 22, 32–3, 36, 90, 08, 108, 111, 116, 127
Audit, 6, 29, 32, 56, 63, 107–8, 110, 128, 136, 141, 153–5

Aus–Meat, 7, 8, 12, 169
Australia, ix, xi, xix–xxi, 1–7, 12, 26, 28, 30–1, 35, 39, 40–3, 45–9, 51, 53–4, 57, 63–4, 79, 95, 110, 120 128, 132, 137–8, 140 160–3, 172–3, 180
  Australian government, 3, 4, 87, 105–7, 163
  Australian Quarantine and Inspection Service (AQIS), 7, 8, 10, 42, 46, 50–1, 53, 65, 87, 144, 146, 149, 154–5

Bahrain, 2, 6, 142, 166
Banking, xvii, 21–2, 97
Barriers (to trade), 19, 70, 122
Beef, 41, 143, 147
Beverages, 3–6, 21, 82, 84–5, 112
Bida, 79,165
Boning room, 9, 10 12, 43, 143, 153
Bonlac foods, 12, 169
Brands (branding), xvii, ix, xix, xx, xxi, 9, 15, 19, 21, 26–7, 30–1, 33, 35, 45–65, 84, 93–120, 172–4, 178–9
Brunei, xix, xxi, 47–8, 93–4, 98, 100–1, 104, 108–14, 117–18, 120, 173
  Government, 100, 104, 109, 110, 113, 120

193

Business enterprises, xvii, xviii, xxii,
    14, 47, 52, 79, 83, 91, 122, 124–5,
    133, 139–40
Butcher, 5, 33, 43

Carcasses, 9, 150
Carton(s), 9, 10, 150–51
Categories of halal consumers, xxi, 13,
    33, 35–6, 38–9
Certifiers (halal), xi, xvii, xviii, xx, 6,
    7, 20, 24–5, 28–9, 31–2, 42, 45,
    49–54, 62–5, 68, 83, 88, 90, 106,
    92, 106, 112, 117, 127–9, 131–3,
    135, 138, 140–2, 144–7, 154,
    146–57, 180
    See also Halal certification, Halal
    certificate & Halal certification
    organisations
Chiller, 9, 150–53
Christianity, xvii, 86, 96
Classification (halal), xvii, 34, 76, 150
Coca–Cola, 94–5, 109
Cold store, 9–10
    See also Freezer & Chiller
Coles Pty Ltd., 30, 31, 43
Competence (halal), 20, 28, 32, 50, 65,
    88, 92, 104, 106, 127–30, 135–6,
    138, 141
    Competent authority, 24, 31, 51, 56,
    58, 62–4
Compliance (halal), xvii–xx, 5, 16, 21,
    30, 37, 42–3, 46, 58, 60, 62–3,
    69–70, 82, 84, 86–7, 91–2, 95,
    101, 104, 106, 111, 115, 119, 122,
    136, 144, 146, 149, 150, 155,157
Concept (halal), xvii–xxii, 3, 4, 13, 19,
    33, 36, 37, 39, 40, 46–8, 51, 54–5,

57–8, 60, 64, 68–77, 82, 84, 93–8,
    105–9, 112, 114, 120, 122, 124,
    130–1, 140
Consumer choice, 14, 33, 35
    Consumerism, 103, 108, 109
Consumer sovereignty, 14–15
Contamination (halal), 26, 84–5, 116,
    149–54,
Contravention (of rules), 25, 84, 105,
    128, 151, 155
Control (halal), xvii, xxi, 5, 6, 29–31, 50,
    56–8, 62–3, 85–7, 90, 105, 110–1,
    115, 119, 123, 136–41, 155, 157,
    160, 166
Conveyor belt, 150–1, 153
Coon (cheese), 31, 179
Cosmetics, xvii, 5, 17–18, 21, 82, 84, 97
Credentials (halal), xxi, 28, 31, 62, 105,
    108, 120, 127, 129, 134, 141, 145
Credibility (halal), xx, 24–5, 28, 31,
    46–7, 54, 59, 61, 65, 67, 83–5, 94,
    102, 104–6, 109, 112, 119
CRF Colac Pty Ltd., xv, 43
Criteria, 32, 52–4, 56, 59, 61–2, 88,
    128–31, 134–6, 141
Customer satisfaction, 15, 22, 68–9,
    70, 99

DEF (Islamic) society, 144–5, 147, 153
Demand, xix, 2, 5–6, 18, 20–1, 38–41,
    44, 67, 68, 79, 86–7, 91, 96–8,
    101, 116, 120, 127, 138, 169
Department of Agriculture... (Aust.),
    41, 171
Department of the Prime Minister
    (Malaysia), 6, 87
Department of Veterinary Services, 6, 87

Index

Disney, 100
Drugs, xii, 4, 5, 73

Education, 21, 52, 106, 126–7, 129, 130, 135–6, 141
Egypt, 160–1
Elders Pty Ltd., 113
Environment, 70, 73, 92, 94, 102–3, 128, 130, 149, 152, 154, 166
Evaluation, 6, 11, 101, 104–9, 112, 119
Exports (halal), xi, xxi, 1, 4, 7, 28, 40–1, 45, 54, 57, 78–9, 90, 125, 148, 156, 159, 160–1, 163, 172
Fatwa, 78, 80–2, 165
Fiqh, 71–2, 165
Food Australia, xvii, 172
Freezer, 10, 150–3

Global halal market, xv–xxii, 1, 4, 16, 18, 20, 25, 67, 69, 101, 120
Girindra, Aisjah, 26, 80–1, 170–1
Goods and services, xv–xviii, 1, 13–16, 18–24, 28, 32, 36, 38–9, 42–4, 46, 62, 68, 70, 76, 84, 122, 125, 166
Grand Metropolitan, 100
Guidelines, 11, 80, 85, 110, 129–31
Gulf Cooperation Council (GCC), 6, 80–2, 142, 166, 169
Guns Pty Ltd., 102

Hadith, 72, 74
Halal approval, xix, 11, 16, 25, 29, 50–1, 56–7, 60–4, 84, 95, 103, 105, 114, 166
Halal authority, 3, 6, 28, 47, 51–2, 63, 84, 87, 106, 115, 133, 138, 148, 166

Halal brand, ix, xi, xvii, xix–xxi, 9, 19, 45–9, 61–65, 93–5, 98, 100, 104–5, 108–20, 173
Halal certification, ix, xi, xvii, xix–xxi, 5, 13, 14, 16, 22–31, 35–6, 39, 41–4, 51–2, 54–61, 89–90, 110, 118, 124–34, 137–41, 144, 156, 166, 177
  Halal certificate, 11, 14, 29, 54–55, 82, 165, 175
  Halal certification organisations, xxi, 130–1, 133–4, 141, 166
  See also Certifiers
Halal community, xx, 121–4, 129, 138
Halal conferences, xviii, 26, 138
Halal Consultative Committee, 45, 49, 65
Halal consumers, xvii, xix, xxi, 13, 15–16, 19, 21–30, 33–40, 42, 44, 58–9, 126
Halal customers, 8, 13, 25, 29, 34, 42, 44, 69, 33, 35–6, 86, 115
Halal development, xvii–xx, 6, 20, 44, 86–7, 92, 96, 108, 112–13, 118, 121, 123–4, 127, 130, 135, 137, 140–1, 170–1
Halal establishment, xv, xviii, xxi, 19, 28, 42–3, 50–51, 60, 83, 144–5, 156–7
Halal export, xxii, 3, 7, 53, 78, 86, 90, 95, 107, 125, 138
Halal food, ix, xi, xvii, 1–7, 12, 17, 21, 67, 87–8, 95–6, 101, 131, 139–41, 156, 166, 169–73
Halal identity, xx, 64, 65, 94, 109, 112
Halal importing countries, 6, 7, 51, 53, 79, 81–2, 88, 113, 123, 125, 148

195

Halal inspection, ix, xxi, 6, 7, 11, 42, 46, 83, 139, 143–7, 154
Halal market, xv– xviii, xxi–xxii, 1, 2, 4, 5, 16, 18, 20, 25, 32, 38, 40 43–4, 61, 67, 69, 101, 120 122, 141, 160, 169–72
Halal meat, 1, 9, 12, 28, 33, 40–2, 45, 49–51, 54–55, 63–4, 79, 82–3, 133, 137, 145, 148, 154, 156, 173
Halal method, xix, xxii
Halal norms and values, xx, 19, 51–2, 59, 62, 64, 70, 78, 83, 85, 97, 111, 115, 125, 135, 161
Halal principles, 69, 81, 83, 85, 91–2, 135–7, 155
Halal products, xvii, xx, 5, 6, 9–10, 12, 16–18, 21, 26–9, 32, 35–6, 38–9, 42, 44, 51–2, 54–61, 67–8, 70, 82, 86, 88, 96, 104, 111, 114, 116, 120 123, 148, 150, 152, 165, 167, 170, 172–3
Halal program, xix, 6, 12, 42, 51, 54, 56, 60–4, 146–50, 156, 166, 182
Halal registration, 52, 55, 88, 148, 154–7, 166
Halal registered (establishment), xix–xxi, 8–9, 12, 28–9, 31, 43, 50–1, 55, 60, 64, 69, 83, 133, 144–5, 148, 153–7,166
Halal requirement, xvii, 3, 8, 10, 11, 20, 28, 43, 149, 155
Halal Research Council, 18, 67, 170–71
Halal rules, 4, 7, 25, 32, 59, 68–70, 75, 77, 81, 83, 84, 90–1, 124, 133, 136, 162
Halal standard, xvii, xviii, xix–xxii, 2, 5, 19, 20, 24, 32, 37, 42, 51, 56, 58–9, 62, 70, 78–84, 90, 92, 95, 105, 111, 115, 118, 122, 124–6, 133, 137, 141, 147–51, 153, 155, 157, 162, 165–6
Halal status, 3, 11, 16, 23–8, 33, 35, 37, 44, 47–8, 51, 54–7, 60–62, 75–6, 82, 84, 110–11, 113, 115, 119, 152, 165
Halal system, 3, 6, 12, 20, 30, 42, 57, 59–60, 81, 87, 90, 101, 105, 110, 118, 127, 129–30, 133–4, 139, 146, 156
Halal trade and commerce, xvii, xviii, xix, xxii, 16, 18–19, 67, 76, 86, 121–7, 135, 138, 141, 172
Haram, xiii, 3–5, 15–16, 18, 25–8, 32, 52, 59, 62–3, 69–77, 79–85, 97, 103, 109, 111, 113–14, 116, 119, 122, 126–8, 133–5, 138, 143, 146, 149–56, 166
Heinz, 100
Hooks, 149–50, 152
Human welfare, 4, 72–3, 92, 97
Hume Leader, 52, 128
Hungry Jacks, 128

Ibadaat, 71, 166
Identity (halal), xix, xx, 2, 8, 15, 18, 21–2, 25, 27, 34–5, 37, 39, 44, 46, 48, 55, 64–5, 94–5, 108–9, 112, 114–19, 132, 135–7, 140, 144, 174
Images, xxi, 15, 159, 170
Indomie, 30–1, 178
Indonesia, ix, xx–xxi, 2, 4, 6, 26, 30–31, 44, 53, 64, 80, 87, 98, 120, 124, 147–9, 159–60, 162–3, 166, 170–3
Ingredients, 4, 11, 26, 29, 82, 110

Index

Disney, 100
Drugs, xii, 4, 5, 73

Education, 21, 52, 106, 126–7, 129, 130, 135–6, 141
Egypt, 160–1
Elders Pty Ltd., 113
Environment, 70, 73, 92, 94, 102–3, 128, 130, 149, 152, 154, 166
Evaluation, 6, 11, 101, 104–9, 112, 119
Exports (halal), xi, xxi, 1, 4, 7, 28, 40–1, 45, 54, 57, 78–9, 90, 125, 148, 156, 159, 160–1, 163, 172
Fatwa, 78, 80–2, 165
Fiqh, 71–2, 165
Food Australia, xvii, 172
Freezer, 10, 150–3

Global halal market, xv–xxii, 1, 4, 16, 18, 20, 25, 67, 69, 101, 120
Girindra, Aisjah, 26, 80–1, 170–1
Goods and services, xv–xviii, 1, 13–16, 18–24, 28, 32, 36, 38–9, 42–4, 46, 62, 68, 70, 76, 84, 122, 125, 166
Grand Metropolitan, 100
Guidelines, 11, 80, 85, 110, 129–31
Gulf Cooperation Council (GCC), 6, 80–2, 142, 166, 169
Guns Pty Ltd., 102

Hadith, 72, 74
Halal approval, xix, 11, 16, 25, 29, 50–1, 56–7, 60–4, 84, 95, 103, 105, 114, 166
Halal authority, 3, 6, 28, 47, 51–2, 63, 84, 87, 106, 115, 133, 138, 148, 166

Halal brand, ix, xi, xvii, xix–xxi, 9, 19, 45–9, 61–65, 93–5, 98, 100, 104–5, 108–20, 173
Halal certification, ix, xi, xvii, xix–xxi, 5, 13, 14, 16, 22–31, 35–6, 39, 41–4, 51–2, 54–61, 89–90, 110, 118, 124–34, 137–41, 144, 156, 166, 177
    Halal certificate, 11, 14, 29, 54–55, 82, 165, 175
    Halal certification organisations, xxi, 130–1, 133–4, 141, 166
    See also Certifiers
Halal community, xx, 121–4, 129, 138
Halal conferences, xviii, 26, 138
Halal Consultative Committee, 45, 49, 65
Halal consumers, xvii, xix, xxi, 13, 15–16, 19, 21–30, 33–40, 42, 44, 58–9, 126
Halal customers, 8, 13, 25, 29, 34, 42, 44, 69, 33, 35–6, 86, 115
Halal development, xvii–xx, 6, 20, 44, 86–7, 92, 96, 108, 112–13, 118, 121, 123–4, 127, 130, 135, 137, 140–1, 170–1
Halal establishment, xv, xviii, xxi, 19, 28, 42–3, 50–51, 60, 83, 144–5, 156–7
Halal export, xxii, 3, 7, 53, 78, 86, 90, 95, 107, 125, 138
Halal food, ix, xi, xvii, 1–7, 12, 17, 21, 67, 87–8, 95–6, 101, 131, 139–41, 156, 166, 169–73
Halal identity, xx, 64, 65, 94, 109, 112
Halal importing countries, 6, 7, 51, 53, 79, 81–2, 88, 113, 123, 125, 148

Halal inspection, ix, xxi, 6, 7, 11, 42, 46, 83, 139, 143–7, 154

Halal market, xv– xviii, xxi–xxii, 1, 2, 4, 5, 16, 18, 20, 25, 32, 38, 40 43–4, 61, 67, 69, 101, 120 122, 141, 160, 169–72

Halal meat, 1, 9, 12, 28, 33, 40–2, 45, 49–51, 54–55, 63–4, 79, 82–3, 133, 137, 145, 148, 154, 156, 173

Halal method, xix, xxii

Halal norms and values, xx, 19, 51–2, 59, 62, 64, 70, 78, 83, 85, 97, 111, 115, 125, 135, 161

Halal principles, 69, 81, 83, 85, 91–2, 135–7, 155

Halal products, xvii, xx, 5, 6, 9–10, 12, 16–18, 21, 26–9, 32, 35–6, 38–9, 42, 44, 51–2, 54–61, 67–8, 70, 82, 86, 88, 96, 104, 111, 114, 116, 120 123, 148, 150, 152, 165, 167, 170, 172–3

Halal program, xix, 6, 12, 42, 51, 54, 56, 60–4, 146–50, 156, 166, 182

Halal registration, 52, 55, 88, 148, 154–7, 166

Halal registered (establishment), xix–xxi, 8–9, 12, 28–9, 31, 43, 50–1, 55, 60, 64, 69, 83, 133, 144–5, 148, 153–7,166

Halal requirement, xvii, 3, 8, 10, 11, 20, 28, 43, 149, 155

Halal Research Council, 18, 67, 170–71

Halal rules, 4, 7, 25, 32, 59, 68–70, 75, 77, 81, 83, 84, 90–1, 124, 133, 136, 162

Halal standard, xvii, xviii, xix–xxii, 2, 5, 19, 20, 24, 32, 37, 42, 51, 56, 58–9, 62, 70, 78–84, 90, 92, 95, 105, 111, 115, 118, 122, 124–6, 133, 137, 141, 147–51, 153, 155, 157, 162, 165–6

Halal status, 3, 11, 16, 23–8, 33, 35, 37, 44, 47–8, 51, 54–7, 60–62, 75–6, 82, 84, 110–11, 113, 115, 119, 152, 165

Halal system, 3, 6, 12, 20, 30, 42, 57, 59–60, 81, 87, 90, 101, 105, 110, 118, 127, 129–30, 133–4, 139, 146, 156

Halal trade and commerce, xvii, xviii, xix, xxii, 16, 18–19, 67, 76, 86, 121–7, 135, 138, 141, 172

Haram, xiii, 3–5, 15–16, 18, 25–8, 32, 52, 59, 62–3, 69–77, 79–85, 97, 103, 109, 111, 113–14, 116, 119, 122, 126–8, 133–5, 138, 143, 146, 149–56, 166

Heinz, 100

Hooks, 149–50, 152

Human welfare, 4, 72–3, 92, 97

Hume Leader, 52, 128

Hungry Jacks, 128

Ibadaat, 71, 166

Identity (halal), xix, xx, 2, 8, 15, 18, 21–2, 25, 27, 34–5, 37, 39, 44, 46, 48, 55, 64–5, 94–5, 108–9, 112, 114–19, 132, 135–7, 140, 144, 174

Images, xxi, 15, 159, 170

Indomie, 30–1, 178

Indonesia, ix, xx–xxi, 2, 4, 6, 26, 30–31, 44, 53, 64, 80, 87, 98, 120, 124, 147–9, 159–60, 162–3, 166, 170–3

Ingredients, 4, 11, 26, 29, 82, 110

Index

Innovation, 43, 79, 165
Inspector, 10, 143, 147–9, 155
Interbrand, 99, 100, 173
Interim/halal certificate, 9–10, 28, 165, 176
Islamic coordinating Council of Australia (ICCA), 7–8, 10–1, 166, 169
Islamic culture, xviii, 126, 162
  Islamic belief, 3, 87
Islamic law and doctrine, xvii, 2–3, 70–2, 74–5, 81, 165–7
Islamic perspective, 20, 35, 40, 55, 58, 61, 69, 79, 81, 84
Islamic Societies, xxi, 45, 49, 51, 53, 82, 85, 87–8, 131–3, 156–7, 173
  Islamic organisation(s), 7, 54, 131
Islamic tradition, 78, 114, 165

Judaism, xvii, 86

Kellogg's, 100
Kosher, xvii, 78–9, 166
Kraft, 99–100
Kuwait, 2, 142, 160, 166

Label (ling), 5–6, 9, 18, 25, 29–31, 35, 60, 82, 85–6, 97, 114, 117, 169–71
Lamb, x, 40–43, 143, 147
Lawful, xiii, xv, 3, 73–6, 169–72
Legitimacy, xx, 16, 46, 60–1, 63–4, 104, 106, 109, 117–20, 155, 161
Logo, 6, 24–5, 29–31, 35, 58, 116–17, 145
L'Oreal, 115

Madhab, 71
Maggi Noodles, 30–1,
Majelis Ulema Indonesia, 6, 26, 31, 80, 87, 166

Makrooh, 76–7, 97, 109, 166
Malaysia, 2, 6, 12, 53, 64, 87, 98, 120, 124, 169, 172
Management (halal), xvii, xxii, 7, 30–1, 84, 86–7, 90, 100, 115–16, 131–2, 135, 137, 141, 149, 152, 150, 166
Marketing, 13–15, 21, 45–8, 54, 56–7, 61, 64, 68, 84, 97, 98, 102–4, 108, 114, 117–18, 141, 169–70, 173
  Marketing tool, 47–8, 54, 84, 117–18
Markets, xxii, 2, 12, 18, 20–1, 25, 28, 30–33, 37–8, 40, 42–4, 61, 75, 78, 86, 116, 116, 125, 161, 169–70
Mashbooh, 74 6, 79, 152, 166
Material world, 3, 69–70, 72, 112, 122
McDonald, 100
Meat and Livestock Australia (MLA), xi, xix–xxi, 45–51, 54–8, 60–5, 160, 170
Melbourne (Australia), xviii, 7, 26, 33, 82, 113, 166, 169–71
Member/ Membership, xx, 45, 50, 55, 61–3, 73, 97, 132–3, 136
Middle East, xvii, 2, 21, 40–1, 45, 142, 170
MLA halal brand, xx, 44, 46, 48–50, 54–8, 60–4
Model, xi, xxi, 6, 43, 46, 48, 63, 90, 100, 109, 125, 128, 130–5, 139, 141
Modern halal consumers, 37, 39
Monitoring, 3, 7, 34, 29, 32, 54, 59, 62, 84, 90, 106–7, 110, 119, 134, 157
Morality, xx, 2–3, 18, 20, 56, 71, 88, 97, 103, 109, 114, 116, 161, 163
Mosque, 7, 31, 134
MS stamp, 9–10, 54
Mua'malat, 71

Muslim countries, xxi, 2–4, 7, 22, 40, 46, 53, 68, 78–9, 86–8, 95, 97, 102–3, 125, 151, 161–2, 171
    Muslim majority countries, xxi, 1–2, 5–6, 34, 41, 116, 152, 156, 160
Muslim Law, xvii, 2–3, 26, 37, 46, 68, 71–5, 77–8, 81–3, 97, 108–9, 143, 148, 166
    See also Islamic law & lawful
Muslim population, 2, 5, 16–18, 86, 89, 101, 169–73
Muslim scholars, 71, 83, 129, 167
Muslim World League (MWL), xv, 64, 140
Mutton, xi, 40–1, 43, 143, 147

Najis, 80, 85
Nescafe', 99
Nestle', 30, 103
New Zealand, xv, 1, 95
Nike, 94, 102
Non–food halal products, xvii, 17, 67, 96
Non–Halal, xix, 9–10, 12, 16, 25–30, 33, 40, 43, 62, 70, 85, 143, 150–1, 153, 167,
Non–Muslim halal consumers, xix, 33–4, 39, 42, 126

Offal, 9
Operations (halal), xvii, 9, 18, 40, 43, 88, 134, 144–9, 153, 155–6
Opportunities (business), xix, xxii, 4, 16, 18–19, 25, 44, 69, 93, 96–7, 121, 170–3

Pew Research Centre, 2, 16, 17, 96, 169–70, 173

Pharmaceutical products, xvii, 5, 17, 21, 82, 84, 97, 115
Phillip Morris, 100
Pillsbury, 100
Pork, 29, 34, 52, 83, 133, 143, 147–9, 154, 156–7
PPP Pty Ltd., ix, 143–45
Product specification, 4, 68, 147
Production (halal), xv, xvii, xx, 1, 11, 22, 25, 28, 44, 55, 58, 63, 68, 83, 86, 144, 146–7, 149, 151, 153–7, 166
Production and processing, 24–5, 28, 146
Professionalism, xxii, 20, 32, 88, 91–2, 101, 123, 127–30, 134–41
Profile, 11, 52, 60, 94–5, 99, 104, 106, 114, 117, 127, 129–30, 136
Prohibited (in Islam), xv, 3–5, 16–18, 70–2, 74–7, 113–14, 143, 166, 169–72
    See also, haram
Promotion, 8, 21, 25, 58, 98, 104, 116–17, 119, 135
Provision of halal services, 7, 24–5, 52, 90, 126–7, 129, 135, 137–8, 140, 144, 145

Qatar, 2, 6, 142, 166

Rails, 9, 149–50, 152
Red meat, 40, 45, 55, 57, 137, 144, 170, 180
Reform, xv, xxi, xxii, 85, 87, 90, 106, 121, 126, 130, 132, 139–40, 161, 173
Regulations, 5, 24, 70, 80–1, 86–7, 90, 118, 136
RMIT University, xviii
Rowntree, 99

Index

Royal Commission, 105, 137, 173
Rubber stamp, ix, xx, xxi, 25, 90, 121, 126–7, 137–9

Sales outcomes, 13, 40, 44, 55, 98
Saudi Arabia, 2, 6, 52–3, 64, 87, 142, 160, 166, 169
Schools of law, 71, 77–8, 82, 166
Senate Inquiry, xxi, 159
Separation (halal), 28, 59, 63, 149–53
Sharia, 2, 5, 24, 26, 28, 32, 37, 46–7, 54, 59, 60–1, 63, 65, 68, 71–2, 74, 78–80, 83, 86, 92, 107, 109, 113, 118–19, 124, 128, 133–4, 136, 141, 143, 148, 152, 166–7
Signage, 29, 151, 153
Singapore, 5, 53, 87, 120, 170–2
Slaughter (halal), 8–10, 12, 29, 34, 51, 54, 59, 75, 78–9, 82, 126–7, 160, 162,
Slaughtermen, 8, 42, 160, 162
Stakeholders, xviii, xx, 28, 111, 122
Storage, 3, 8–9, 28, 59, 152–3, 156, 165
Strategic interest, 2, 18
Structure (certification), xi, xxi, 7, 20, 52, 89, 106, 119, 129, 138, 140–2
Stun free slaughter, 78–9, 161
Stunning, 8–9, 78–9, 160, 162
Sub–categories (halal consumers), 35, 38, 42
Sunna (Islamic tradition), 2, 4, 71, 74, 113, 167
Supermarkets, xxii, 30–1, 33, 42–3
Supervision, 7, 10, 24, 29, 32, 54, 58–9, 62, 106, 110, 134, 145–6, 153–5
  Halal supervisor, 9, 42, 145, 153–4
Symbol, 29, 51, 55, 59–61, 64, 116–17

Tasmania, 102
The Halal Journal, xx
Transparency, xxii, 52, 129
Transportation, 3, 8–10

Ulema, 87, 105, 122, 167
Uniform (halal) standard, 3, 20, 24, 52, 70–1, 78, 80–2, 90–1, 105, 107, 118, 124–6, 140–1
Unilever, 103, 114
United Arab Emirates (UAE), xx, 6, 26, 41, 44, 53, 64, 87, 166
University of Melbourne, xviii
Universality, xxi, xxii, 3, 20, 33, 37–8, 49, 60, 77–8, 82, 91–2, 105, 107, 110, 117–19, 122, 124–6, 135, 140–1

Validation, 3, 16, 22–5, 28–31, 35, 38, 46–9, 54, 56–9, 63–4, 67–8, 70, 75–6, 78, 81–7, 95, 104–7, 109, 111, 113, 115, 119, 127, 137, 138, 144–6, 149, 156, 160–2, 165
Verifiability, 25, 59

Weaknesses in certification, xx, xxi, 23–4, 52, 90, 137, 156
Western countries, 2, 5, 13, 21, 28, 30, 33, 35, 42, 67, 78–9, 87, 95, 103, 130–1
Woolworths, 30, 43
World Halal Food Council (WHFC), 139–40
World Halal Forum, 17
World view, 18, 161

www.ingramcontent.com/pod-product-compliance
Lightning Source LLC
Chambersburg PA
CBHW061505180526
45171CB00001B/50